Growth Through Nature

A Preschool Program for Children with Disabilities

Based on a program developed by the Enid A. Haupt Glass Garden

at the Rusk Institute of Rehabilitation Medicine,

in collaboration with the Preschool at Rusk Institute

Growth Through Nature

A Preschool Program for Children with Disabilities

Stephanie L. Molen ❧ Nancy K. Chambers

Matthew J. Wichrowski ❧ Gwenn Fried

edited by Harvey Loomis ❧ illustrated by Vincent Chiu

SAGAPRESS, INC. ❧ SAGAPONACK, NEW YORK

Published in 1999 by Sagapress, Inc., Sagaponack, New York
Distributed by Timber Press, Inc., Portland, Oregon

Design and composition by Wilsted & Taylor Publishing Services
Production coordinated by Carol Lewis

Printed in the United States of America

Library of Congress Cataloging-in-Publication Data
Growth through nature : a preschool program for children with
    disabilities / by Stephanie L. Molen ... [et al.]. ; edited by
    Harvey Loomis ; illustrated by Vincent Chiu ; based on a program
    developed by the Enid A. Haupt Glass Garden at the Rusk Institute of
    Rehabilitation Medicine, in collaboration with the preschool at Rusk
    Institute.
        p.   cm.
      ISBN 0-89831-042-3 (pbk.)
        1. Handicapped children—Education (Preschool)—United States—
    Curricula Case studies.   2. Nature study—Study and teaching
    (Preschool)—United States—Curricula Case studies.   3. Education,
    Preschool—Activity programs—United States Case studies.   4. Nature
    and nurture—United States Case studies.   I. Molen, Stephanie L.
    II. Loomis, Harvey.   III. Enid A. Haupt Glass Garden.
    LC4019.2.G76   1999
    371.95'33'57—dc21   99-21559
                                                            CIP

CONTENTS

Acknowledgments   9

INTRODUCTION   11

HOW DISABILITIES AFFECT
DEVELOPMENT   15

PUTTING THE PROGRAM TO WORK   19

THE LESSON PLANS   27

Planting

lesson 1: Soil and Sand   28
*This activity should be the first lesson, as it is the basis for most of the
planting lessons.*

lesson 2: Propagating Jade   30
Use this lesson or the next, Propagating Kalanchoe, *as the follow-up to
Soil and Sand.*

lesson 3: Propagating Kalanchoe   32
*Horticultural concepts will be reinforced through repetition of similar
activities.*

lesson 4: Propagating Scented Geranium Cuttings   34
*This lesson on stem propagation can be used as the children become more
familiar with handling plants.*

Seeds

lesson 5: Collecting Pumpkin Seeds   36
This lesson is the cornerstone for all pumpkin seed lessons. Autumn is the best time of year for the pumpkin series.

lesson 6: Planting Pumpkin Seeds   38
This lesson will naturally follow the harvesting of the seeds.

lesson 7: Examining Pumpkin Seedlings   40
This activity is an ongoing observation experience as children examine the seedlings over a period of time.

lesson 8: Creating a Pumpkin Seed Picture   42
This activity will be more meaningful if preceded by the previous pumpkin lessons.

lesson 9: Decorating Mini-Pumpkins   44
This activity can be used to reinforce horticultural concepts from previous lessons.

Bulbs

lesson 10: Planting Paperwhite Bulbs   46
This experience with planting paperwhites is a natural introduction to the lessons on tulip planting.

lesson 11: Planting Tulip Bulbs (Indoors)   48
Tulip bulbs planted in pots can be later planted outdoors, and will allow the forcing of the tulips in the spring.

lesson 12: Planting Tulip Bulbs (Outdoors)   50
This activity is seasonal and begins the children's observations of the garden at different times of year.

Kitchen Gardening

lesson 13: Recipe for Good Earth   52
It is never too early to learn about taking care of our world.

lesson 14: Planting Potatoes   54
Potato eyes are fast growers and fun to watch daily.

lesson 15: Planting Carrot Tops   56
Using "kitchen scraps" can be fun.

lesson 16: Planting an Avocado Pit   58
Tasting avocado meat may be a new experience.

lesson 17: Collecting Citrus Seeds   60
Harvesting seeds from citrus fruits will add to children's knowledge of plant parts.

lesson 18: Planting Citrus Seeds   62
Waiting for seeds to germinate requires patience.

lesson 19: Transplanting Citrus Seedlings 64

Transplanted seedlings are slow growers.

Roots

lesson 20: Propagation by Division 66

The root development of a plant is important to this lesson.

lesson 21: Aloe Vera Propagation 68

Plants are grown and used for medicine.

lesson 22: Spider Plant Propagation 70

The comparison of spider plants to household spiders is obvious.

lesson 23: Pothos Propagation 72

This lesson can be used any time of year.

Flowers

lesson 24: Collecting Sunflower Seeds 74

Collecting sunflower seeds demonstrates that flowers produce seeds.

lesson 25: Planting Sunflower Seeds 76

This lesson will build upon previous lessons. Sunflower seeds germinate quickly.

lesson 26: Transplanting Sunflower Seedlings 78

Children will be able to watch their seedlings grow to maturity.

lesson 27: Making Sunflower Seed Pictures 80

This lesson will be more meaningful if preceded by previous sunflower lessons.

Specific Plant Projects

lesson 28: Transplanting Micro-Tom Tomatoes 82

Children will be able to harvest the fruit of the plants.

lesson 29: Transplanting Flowering Geraniums 84

This activity can be combined with Lesson 40, Making Gift Tags with Pressed Flowers.

lesson 30: Planting Grass Seeds 86

Seeds can be sown directly into prepared soil outdoors, if planting space is available and accessible.

lesson 31: Planting Seeds in Plastic Eggs 88

This activity can be combined with Lesson 30, Planting Grass Seeds.

Horticulture Crafts

lesson 32: Holiday Nut Baskets 90

This craft activity continues to enrich the children's knowledge of seeds.

lesson 33: Painting Pine Cones   92

This lesson combines natural material with the creative process of painting.

lesson 34: Creating Pine Cone Nests   94

This craft activity is especially appropriate for a holiday decoration.

lesson 35: Making a Pine Cone Bird Feeder   96

Use this activity to help the children become aware of their natural environment. Good for a winter excursion.

lesson 36: Making Grapevine Picture Frames   98

This project is appropriate for any time of year.

lesson 37: Creating Fresh Green Centerpieces   100

Creativity abounds with this project. Can be used for holidays.

lesson 38: Building Birds' Nests   102

This project is especially meaningful when the children can collect some of the material needed to build the nests.

lesson 39: Pressing Flowers   104

This lesson works best when the children have experience with identification of plant parts.

lesson 40: Making Gift Tags with Pressed Flowers   106

This activity reinforces Lesson 39, Pressing Flowers.

APPENDIX

Glossary   108

Suppliers   111

Bibliography   112

About the Authors   114

ACKNOWLEDGMENTS

Without the dedication and contributions of many colleagues and associates, this book would never have been created. We are privileged to acknowledge the following individuals and organizations for their foresightedness and their faith in the Rusk Preschool Nature Program.

Our foremost thanks go to the professionals at the Rusk Institute preschool: Dr. Stephen M. Bicchieri, Principal, and teachers Linda Fuller and Joanne McClement. They, and their dedicated staff, gave us their full support and assistance so that we could try out this nature program in their classrooms. The children were our inspiration.

Special thanks go to Phyllis Hollander, a Glass Garden volunteer, who worked closely with Stephanie Molen in implementing this program. Phyllis provided a valuable sounding board as well as encouragement and enthusiasm.

We are very grateful to those who contributed to, commented on and reviewed the text, including Sharon Lee, Phyllis D'Amico, Mary Leou, JoAnn Singband, Lotte Kunstler, Lauri Dien, and Dr. Ruth Wilson. They helped keep us focused and on track.

Ngaere Macray, publisher of Sagapress, made us believe we could write a book. She pushed and made sure we completed it. Harvey Loomis will always be remembered as our dear editor.

Thanks to the Garden Club of New York, whose initial donation provided grow carts for each classroom. Thanks also to Donald Molen, whose advocacy on behalf of the children's programs generated financial support from the partnership of J. Streicher and Co. and from members of the American Stock Exchange.

Most particularly, we are grateful to the Pinkerton Foundation, which gave us a grant for this entire project.

And to all of the people before us who understood and wrote about the importance of nature experiences in children's development: Thank you!

Introduction

Jennifer is a very attractive four-year-old with cerebral palsy. When we first met Jennifer four months ago she was shy and withdrawn. Although she could stand and walk with the help of a walker, she didn't play with other children in the classroom. She usually sat passively at the table, and refused to touch the soil or sand or flowers in front of her. She would not put her fingers in the watering can to touch the water. But she did watch the teacher closely and allowed her to softly touch her cheek with a rose.

Today, Jennifer passes plants, soil, and watering cans to the children next to her. She uses her hands to stir the soil and sand mixture in which to plant her succulent cutting. She calls out the answers to the teacher, correctly identifying roots and flower and stem. Jennifer loves to water her own plant and enjoys the feel of the overflow dribbling on her fingers. She is no longer afraid of getting dirty or of touching new things. She is an active participant in class, learning new skills and vocabulary. She laughs and has fun, just as a four-year-old should.

Jennifer is one of 18 participants in a special nature program that the horticulture staff of the Enid A. Haupt Glass Garden at Rusk Institute of Rehabilitation Medicine offers once a week to the public preschool classes housed at Rusk Institute in New York City. This nursery school is an early intervention program, funded by the New York State Department of Education. Its mission is to provide individualized educational and therapeutic services for children ages three to five who have orthopedic and other disabilities or delayed development.

Their disabilities may be those associated with cerebral palsy, spina bifida, neurological impairment, brain injury, or other traumas. All the children have disabilities that affect muscle movement and coordination. They need both physical and occupational therapy, and most require speech therapy. In addition, because of their disabilities, they are already behind in learning and development when they enter the preschool. Jennifer is one of these children.

Our nature program uses hands-on activities to stimulate sensory, motor, cognitive, and communication skills in children like Jennifer. It introduces horticulture projects to increase knowledge and awareness of nature and develop early science learning. It encourages the children to respond to the wonders and beauty of nature and instills in them positive feelings about the earth and their place in it.

For most children such an intensive introduction to nature is not necessary. At the youngest ages, normal children rely on touching, feeling, and other senses as well as muscle movements to gather and interpret information about the world. These children are active learners, manipulating objects and coordinating movements to develop an understanding of their environment and their relationship with it. Even urban children create a "sense" of and connection to the natural world quite early through play, by rolling on the ground, crawling under shrubs, jumping in puddles, smelling the earth, feeling the sun's heat and the wind, touching insects, stones, dirt, and water.

But each year in the United States approximately 150,000 babies are born with birth defects that prevent them from achieving this connection with nature, and another 230,000 become disabled at some point during childhood. Some, like Jennifer, have restricted mo-tor abilities and reduced endurance, which limits their opportunity to interact, experience, and play, especially outside in nature. Others have sensory or perceptual deficits and are unable to integrate or accurately organize the colors, lights, shapes, sounds, and textures their senses receive.

Generally, children with such disabilities are more sheltered than most. They are often confined to wheelchairs, and are less spontaneous in play. For these children, play occurs most often indoors, with man-made, "safe" materials and objects, rather than with grass, puddles, and trees. These children have fewer chances to experience nature and often become passive observers, learning about nature in the abstract through books, movies, or television. As a consequence, they are at risk of never bonding with the natural world. They often become fearful of "dirt," "bugs," and "goo," and can develop negative attitudes toward the environment and the natural world. That is what had happened to Jennifer.

This book is a guide to various strategies developed in 1995 by members of the staff of the Enid A. Haupt Glass Garden to help children like Jennifer overcome their fear and passivity. We believe all children need to interact actively with nature to develop positive attitudes toward the environment, for their own sake, and to prepare them to be future stewards of the earth. Moreover, we are convinced that it is important to foster these attitudes as early as possible in their lives, when lifelong values and beliefs about the world are formed.

To that end, we have designed this book to introduce nature lessons in an easy, practical way for teachers, parents, and therapists who teach and treat young disabled children. It is meant to offer new ideas for reaching preschool children with special needs in order to enhance all their learning processes. It offers diverse experiences, using nature's materials, that prompt children to use all their senses—to observe and manipulate soil, sand, seeds, roots, stems, leaves, flowers, and water.

These hands-on activities will help children develop an understanding about the natural world and their connection to it by observing and handling nature's shapes, textures, sizes, weights, and colors. Simultaneously, they are building fine motor and coordination skills, learning to share, and developing language and communication proficiency by using vocabulary that describes what they see and feel. The overall effect, we hope and believe, is to help children develop initiative, curiosity, confidence, responsibility, and independence.

In developing the program, we have linked child development theory, rehabilitation, and environment/nature education with sound educational practice and proven therapeutic intervention. Moreover, our faith in the program is bolstered by our experience. The program at Rusk has been remarkably successful. In the beginning, when the garden program conflicted with individually scheduled speech, occupa-

tional, or physical therapy sessions, these other therapies were given priority by the clinical staff. After a few months, however, therapists recognized the benefits of the nature program, and began to adjust the children's schedules so that the children could attend their nature classes. In fact, the therapists often participated with the children in the garden program, to enhance and augment the clinical aspects of each child's participation.

While refining the program, we looked for theoretical underpinnings in the literature of environmental and nature studies, and in special education and early education fields. We discovered that there is almost no published information about nature programs for preschool children with disabilities. Other environmental programs start their curriculums at kindergarten age and focus on children who already have significant cognitive, language, and motor skills. These programs deal with children who are able to understand simple abstract concepts such as comparing, who can focus on an activity for more than 30 seconds, who have the ability to talk to each other, and also are unafraid to touch water or soil or a leaf. The children we were trying to help had none of those skills.

So we set out to document our own discoveries and to experience and clarify our procedures in a way that might be useful to others. This guide is the result, and we gladly dedicate it to teachers, therapists, parents, and others who work with children with disabilities.

How Disabilities Affect Development

Infants begin moving long before birth. Once out of the womb, movement propels the child into experiences with people and things that begin the process of learning. The interaction of these external factors with the child's own maturing process result, over time, in development. This development proceeds as an interrelated whole, with all aspects—physical, social, emotional, cognitive—influencing the others. But when children are born with disabilities, the process of maturation as well as the opportunities for external engagement are diminished. This decreases their chances of achieving full potential.

The factors that cause significant development problems in children can occur before, during, and after birth. Internal factors such as recessive disorders and chromosomal abnormalities, and external factors such as the age of the mother, prenatal nutrition problems, drug use, and certain diseases contracted by the mother during pregnancy can cause later disabilities in a child. Anoxia during birth, in-fant head trauma, exposure to neurotoxins such as lead, and central nervous system infections and trauma can also disable a young child. Effects of these disabling factors on growth vary greatly, but it is clear that they all impair a child's development and well-being.

Physical Issues

Since movement, especially in the early years, is inseparable from learning, any diminution of mobility can translate into lost learning opportunities that, if not addressed, can eventually create secondary disabilities. Children with cerebral palsy may exhibit abnormally high or low muscle tone resulting in extreme rigidity or weakness; individuals with spina bifida may be confined to wheelchairs due to their weakly developed lower extremities. Sensory or perceptual disorders can drastically change the way a child moves through space and experiences the world.

cerebral palsy may feel stiff or unresponsive to parents because of their high muscle tension and may be slower to respond to parents' attempts to engage them in play.

Infants who are premature or have low birth weight or other health problems such as bronchopulmonary dysplasia may be fussy and may tire easily during play. Prenatal exposure to drugs may cause infants to be irritable and display irregular sleep patterns. Any of these problems can lead preschool children with disabilities to be more solitary and less social than their non-disabled peers. This isolation will almost certainly affect the development of a child's social skills.

Cognitive and Language Issues

In addition to the physical and social difficulties experienced by disabled children, their cognitive abilities may also suffer, depending on the amount of damage and the area of the brain affected. Overall, children with disabilities develop intellectually in much the same way as non-disabled children, but they are likely to take longer to do so and, in some instances, may display qualitative differences as well. Cognitive functions that disabled children may have difficulty with vary greatly: length of attention span; short- and long-term memory; the ability to anticipate consequences and to carry out activities or solve problems, to learn vocabulary, to acquire language and counting skills.

Social and Emotional Issues

Being disabled can also greatly affect children's ability to socialize. The first indication of this is in a child's interaction with his or her parents. An infant with visual impairment may have a muted smile and may show her interest in interacting with her parents in ways that are hard for them to interpret. The smile of a baby with Down's syndrome may be less engaging for his parents than smiles of non-disabled infants and can cause their interaction to be less ardent. Infants with

Benefits of Nature Education Activities

One of the important goals for disabled children—and particularly of the nature program described here—is to provide materials and activities that require them to work together in social groups, to learn to take turns, assist others, and practice appropriate communication. As with all children, those with disabilities benefit from an environment that provides opportunities for sensorimotor stimulation and instructional guidance from an adult. The development of self-esteem is fostered when situations are structured so that children can succeed, when the right amount of help is offered for success, when efforts to understand communication are made, and when children's advice is solicited and their opinions respected.

Since young children learn primarily through their senses and through motor manipulation, they are excellent candidates for nature education experiences. Nature activities engage all their senses and provide common experiences embedded to some degree in most people's lives. Children's gross motor skills are exercised as they perform the varied whole-body movements required to participate in the activities described in this nature program. Outdoor activities encourage a wide range of physical movements as children walk, climb, dig, plant, or roll on the grass. Indoors, fine motor skills are exercised through the manipulation of the variously sized objects used in the lesson plans. Strength, range of motion, and perceptual skills are all used in filling pots with soil, reaching for or passing supplies and tools, lifting a watering can, and forming patterns with cuttings or seeds.

Besides developing physical capacities, the nature program also provides rich opportunities for improving social abilities. The program fosters group work, cooperation, consideration for others, and sharing. Group activities encourage children to interact, and allow the teacher to assist by introducing and modeling appropriate social behavior when opportunities present themselves. The group also allows for a mix of peer abilities in which less skilled individuals can benefit from the example of more advanced members. Success with their projects enhances self-esteem. Caring for the needs of a living plant can foster empathy and a greater awareness of one's own needs.

Many areas of cognitive development are stimulated by the vast array of sensory qualities present in nature. All the senses can be engaged and stimulated: *sight*, by the form, shape, color, and contrast of natural objects such as leaves, fruits, flowers, vegetables, stones; *hearing*, through the rustling of leaves, seed pods, the rattle of dried gourds; *smell*, with fragrant flowers, aromatic herbs, and fresh-cut grass; *touch*, by the full spectrum of textures present in the plant world; *taste*, through the many fruits, vegetables, and herbs that children can be introduced to during class. All these elements provide a wide-ranging repertoire of sensory-motor stimulation available to the astute teacher and developing child. Opportunities for play abound in a nature activities setting, whether indoors or out. Size, shape, texture, numbers, and contrasting concepts such as light and heavy, empty and full, can be explored using interesting objects with a high motivational factor.

In short, as Dr. Ruth Wilson puts it, "The world's greatest language development kit is the world itself." Under the guidance of a knowledgeable instructor, the natural world and activities using nature's materials provide a rich array of ideally suited educational opportunities for our children—disabled or not.

Putting the Program to Work

As you begin your adventure into the natural world with your young charges, the lesson plans will guide you in selection of activities. You may choose, as we do, to tackle one lesson each week. The plans increase in difficulty and build on skills and vocabulary as the school year progresses from September into the summer months. You can, however, with some preparation, use any of the lessons in whatever order fits your curriculum best. In this chapter you will find an inventory of specific items you'll need to execute the lesson plans that follow, as well as more general suggestions to help you successfully run and enhance your nature program.

Setting Up the Program

First, you will need some basic supplies. Many items are common household goods, available in hardware stores, discount stores, and garden centers. Some sources for more selective items are listed in the Appendix of this manual. Recycling common household items will lower the program cost—and teach environmental responsibility as well.

Here is what you'll need:

1. A *windowsill* or a shelf near a window is necessary for observation of the plants. Try to make the observation area easily accessible to the children to invite them to witness nature at work. Trays placed under the plants will avoid ruining the finish on the shelf.

2. *Soil:* We use the word "soil," but actually we recommend a soil-less mix of peat moss and perlite. The texture of the soil is important, because the children should enjoy touching it. Soil should be kept in a covered container so it does not dry out.

3. A *plastic basin* 10"–12" in diameter, for each child, is suggested, to allow everyone to have an individual supply of soil.

4. *Water.*

5. *Watering cans:* Small cans— 1- or 1½-pint—with long spouts and easy-to-grasp handles are best. Encourage children

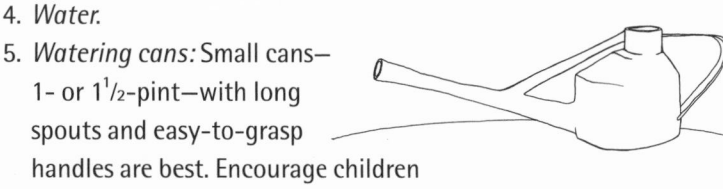

to use the watering cans, even if they need to be helped; children who cannot handle a watering can should use a sponge for watering.

6. *Pots:* 4" square white pots, or small azalea pots (3½"-tall round pots), one for each child, are recommended unless another size is specified in the lesson plan. It's a good idea to print the children's names on the pots, which helps in name recognition.

7. *Plastic plant saucers* (6" size) should be put under the pots during watering.

8. *Plastic plant labels* that are large enough for the children to see and handle can be used to write the name of each plant and the date it is planted.

9. *Permanent markers* with fine points.

10. A *tarp* to cover the floor under the table. There will be, and should be, a mess.

11. A *round table* is recommended rather than a rectangular one, to aid in interaction and to give the teacher eye contact with each child.

12. A *table cover* is suggested; or you may use *individual trays* that are large enough to hold a soil basin with extra space for the child to work in.

13. *Scoops* for filling the pots with soil. Ice cream scoops with thick handles work well. Get them in different colors so the children can choose their own colors.

14. *Dibbles* are needed to make holes for planting. A dibble is any stick that you can use to make a hole in the soil. Round chopsticks work well.

15. Small *scissors* will be useful if the children have enough dexterity to use them.

16. Thin *rubber bands.*

17. Pint-size *spray bottles* are needed for misting.
18. *Name tags* for the students who do not already have them.
19. *Plant materials* as listed in the lesson plans.

The Lesson Plans

The lesson plans are designed to take you through the year, beginning in September and continuing with one per week for 40 weeks. As the year progresses, the lessons build upon previously acquired skills and initiate group participation in activities, in addition to activities that are completed individually. The repetition of procedures and vocabulary throughout the year assists children by building their confidence and familiarity.

Whether you follow the seasonal format of these lesson plans or pick and choose individual lessons throughout the year, you will see that each lesson plan lists various objectives that the activity will promote. The areas of growth will be in sensory motor areas, language and vocabulary development, physical dexterity, social interaction, and cognition.

Activity and Process

As you look at individual lesson plans, analyze the activity to be sure that it attains the goals that you have set for the children. Remember that in all activities "the process" is the beneficial part of the plan, and that completion of the activity or the perfect product may be secondary or even unnecessary.

Be aware of the benefit of the group process. Having the children pass items to one another and taking turns are great ways to introduce children to one another and to reinforce name recognition. It will also foster sharing and cooperative learning and will promote friendship.

Horticultural Practices and Vocabulary

Unless directed otherwise, the procedures listed below are the recommended horticultural practices to use when following the lesson plans:

• *Filling the pot.* The 4" square white pot used for most potting activities should be filled to the line on the inside of the pot, or one half-inch from the top, to leave room for watering. The soil should be well packed. Use a scoop, hands, or the bottom of another pot to press the soil down.

- *Watering the plant.* Most plants should be watered slowly, from the top, until the water leaks from the holes at the bottom of the pot. The water should be allowed to drain into the saucer and then the saucer should be emptied. Never allow the plant to sit in the saucer of water. To help a child manipulate the watering can, try using the "hand-over-hand" technique: put your hand on top of the child's hand while lifting and pouring.

- *Using a dibble.* In order to make a hole for planting a seed or cutting when propagating a plant, place the dibble in the soil and push it to the bottom of the pot. Keeping the bottom of the dibble stable, rotate it until you form a hole of the right size; the hole must be large enough to accommodate the diameter of the stem. Twist the dibble and remove it from the soil.

- *Propagating a plant.* Propagation is any activity in which a new plant is created. The lesson plans include propagation from seed, stem cutting, and division. Each is fully explained in the plan.

- *Removing a plant from a pot.* To get a plant out of a pot for division or transplanting, have each child squeeze the pot. This will release the plant from the sides of the pot and make it easier to remove. If the plant is large, place the pot on its side on a tray and let the children take turns pressing on the pot.

- *Moistening the soil.* If any of the children in the group have respiratory problems, thoroughly moisten the soilless mix and allow the children to add some dry mix on top. The children can observe the difference between wet and dry, or light and dark. But don't let the children scoop the dry mix because the dust created may cause breathing problems.

- *Keeping supplies handy.* It is a big help to keep all the supplies you will use regularly on a cart that can be rolled up near the table during the lessons. The supplies necessary for almost all activities are soil, pots, water, watering cans, soil basins, dibbles, markers, and labels.

- *Definitions*

    Germination. When starting plants from seed, the date that you see green plant material above the soil is the date of germination.

    Petiole. The petiole is the slender stalk by which the leaf is attached to the stem.

    Node. The node is the point at which the leaf petiole is attached to the stem.

Time to Begin

Before starting each activity, allow the students to discover something new about nature; spontaneity and creativity can lead you down unsuspected and enjoyable paths. But if structure is necessary, then your introductory experience should be directly related to your current lesson. In either case, this will be a natural way to focus the attention of the children and make them aware of the others in the group and the exciting activity about to begin. Suggestions for basic introductory activities are offered at the beginning of each lesson plan.

Lessons can be made more challenging for the children by limiting your own advance preparation, or made easier by doing more yourself ahead of time. Expand the lesson plans to meet the needs of your children. Math concepts (counting, measuring, comparing) can be easily integrated into each lesson; science skills (observing, questioning, testing) can also be assimilated.

Most of the lesson plans are designed to be conducted indoors, but some of them are specifically tailored for use outdoors. Gardening outside gives you the obvious benefits of natural surroundings: sunlight, fresh air and exercise, observation of the changing seasons. A year-round program gives you a chance to interact with nature on a daily basis, to the extent that your climate allows. You can start with a window box, or you may want to have border plantings or actual garden plots. Of course, taking the class outdoors presents logistical problems; the important things are to be sure your outdoor area has accessible walkways to ensure that all of the children can participate, and that there are no dangers for them in the environment (see Safety Issues below).

Plants chosen for an outside garden should encourage use of different senses. Herbs that have different scents, brightly colored plants, textured plants, and plants with interesting growth habits and winter interest, like colorful bark, will engage students and teachers alike. Most importantly, be sure that you schedule some unstructured time during the program for the children to experience nature through their own eyes, at their own speed, and in their own way.

Adding On

Once your program gets underway, you will doubtless begin to think of ways to add new dimensions. Ideally, your wish list should include an outdoor garden designed specifically for your children's use. Building such a garden can be a major project, or you can just begin with some simple containers and take off from there.

house you need, where it would be built, and how you will handle problems of accessibility. Some possible suppliers for greenhouses are listed in the Appendix.

A much more attainable item that will enhance your nature program is a light cart. This is a self-contained unit that has two to three shelves with trays for plants with adjustable fluorescent lights mounted above each shelf. Carts can be bought from a number of suppliers, but if the cost is beyond your budget, you can build a satisfactory substitute by buying shelves and hanging fluorescent fixtures about three inches above the plants.

Grants are available for buying light carts as well as greenhouses. Look toward environmentally minded foundations and children's charities for this funding. Talk to other people who have done similar programs in your area and to local community-minded businesses. The American Horticultural Therapy Association, located in Gaithersburg, Maryland, administers an annual greenhouse grant program, and National Gardening, in Burlington, Vermont, gives annual grants for children's gardening program supplies. You can contact them for applications.

If cost is a major issue in setting up the program, it is wise to minimize your initial supply purchase and add to your inventory in small installments. Also, it may be easier than you think to solicit donations of plants and materials from local growers, neighbors, parents, horticultural societies, clubs, and botanical gardens. Always be aware,

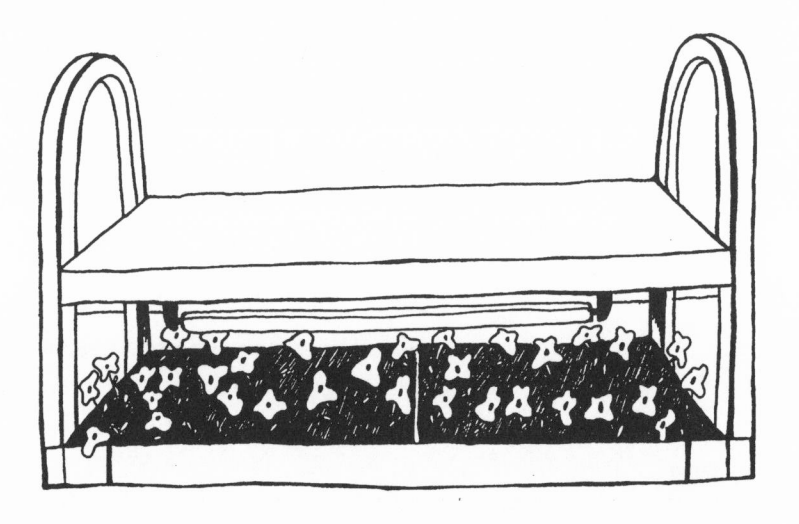

Another major enhancement to your program would be a greenhouse that provides all-weather access to a controlled natural environment. This requires a serious commitment by administration and staff, but it is not an impossible goal; prices and styles of greenhouses vary greatly, and grants for buying greenhouses are available. Before you begin looking for funding, though, figure out how big a green-

though, of the possibility that chemical pesticides may have been used on plants; it is important to accept only safe donations. Quality products reflect a quality program and a quality program will elicit increased donations.

Safety Issues

Safety issues are especially important whenever children with disabilities are involved. When inside, be sure to take precautions with sharp tools, do not use any chemicals, use only non-poisonous plants and materials, and cover any open wounds on children before beginning a project. Keep child-sized gloves and Band-Aids available. Staff your classes suitably by using teacher's aides and parent volunteers when available. It is imperative, though, when the program is administered by anyone other than the classroom teacher that the teacher remains and participates. This helps keep the children focused and feeling safer and more comfortable.

Outdoor safety precautions are similar. First, be sure that your activity takes place in an enclosed area. Keep close control of tools and be sure that no chemicals are in use by anyone who is maintaining the outdoor space. Check for toxicity of other plants in the area and verify the condition of play equipment in the space. Be sure the area is well drained. Plan an interactive space that summons the child to enter and enjoy, but take into account the additional supervision that may be needed. Again, take advantage of aides and parent volunteers.

Finally, when using this program be aware that each child will participate on a different level. One may be able to finish a task with relatively little assistance while another may need constant help and a third may not be able to finish the assignment at all. Attention span may dictate that the activity be spread over a two-day period. You often will need to adapt lessons while they are in progress. Many learning opportunities cannot be anticipated, but if you are flexible, seizing on them when they occur will become second nature as you spend more time with the children. And never forget that your most important goal is to help the children build a bond with nature.

We hope this book will provide you with a key to open the world of nature to your students. Its curriculum is just a stepping stone to learning; use it with imagination, and the sky's your limit.

The Lesson Plans

lesson 1   Soil and Sand

This activity should be the first lesson, as it is the basis for most of the planting lessons.

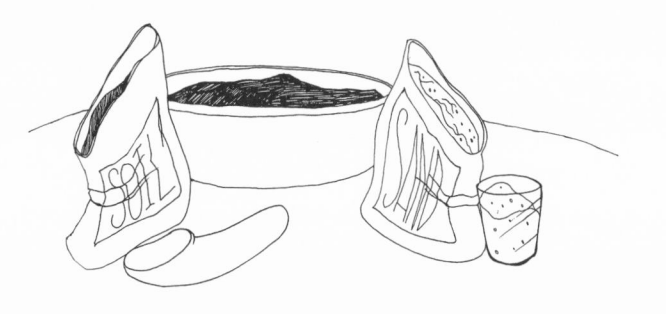

materials
Basins or trays, soil mixture, 4" azalea pots, sand, ice cream scoops, permanent markers, 4-oz. cups.

preparation
For each child:
1. Fill basin or tray with approximately 1 qt. of soil.
2. Fill 4-oz. cups $1/2$ to $3/4$ full with sand.
3. Place cup of sand in basin.
4. Write each child's name with marker on a pot.
5. Prepare activity area.

procedures
1. *Introduction:* The outdoor garden is abundant with flowering plants. Bring some soft-petalled flowers that you can rub against the cheeks or arms of the children. Explain that these are flowers and that flowers grow in soil.
2. Pass teacher's basin with soil around table, encouraging each child to feel soil.
3. Pass basin of sand around table, encouraging each child to touch sand.
4. Demonstrate to children the incorporation of the sand into soil, mixing with hands or scoop.
5. Demonstrate filling the "sandy soil" to the line inside the pot.
6. Have children pass basins around the table.
7. Tell children to pour sand into soil.
8. Exchange each child's empty cup for a scoop. They can pick their own color.
9. Mix sand and soil with children.
10. Pass pots from child to child and have children fill their pots with "sandy soil" mix.

problems
This is the first class in the horticulture sequence. Children's attention spans vary widely and some may not stay in or with the group. Some

children may not want to touch the soil. There will be a wide range of physical abilities and some children may need hand-over-hand assistance.

adaptations
Many of the children will function best with one-on-one attention from an adult. Encourage the use of scoops for those who do not want to handle the soil. Soil basins will be appropriate for some children; others, who cannot pick their arms up over the basins' sides, will need trays, which are flatter, to hold the soil.

hints to maximize benefits
Give children one tool at a time to do one step at a time. This is the first step in the plant propagation sequence that they will be following in many of the lessons. Begin the first session with the children passing material to one another as you say each child's name. They will begin to recognize others in the group.

developmental processes
· Practice attending skills
· Follow one-step directions
· Practice social interaction skills
· Exercise sensory-motor skills
· Experience tactile sensations, i.e., sandy, smooth

nature concepts and processes
· Introduce soil.
· Introduce sand.
· When sand and soil are mixed together, we make "sandy soil."
· Compare full and empty pot.

vocabulary
· *sand* · *soil* · *scoop* · *basin* · *mix* · *fill* · *pot* · *full* · *empty* · *heavy*
· *light* · *sandy*

lesson 2 Propagating Jade

Use this lesson, or the lesson *Propagating Kalanchoe*, as the follow-up lesson to *Soil and Sand*.

materials
Soil, sand, basins or trays, 4-oz. cups, 4″ pots, jade plant to take cuttings, 4″–6″ jade cuttings, jade leaves; scoops, watering cans with water, saucers, dibbles, scissors, permanent marker, labels.

preparation
1. Take stem cuttings from a jade plant. Cuttings should have 3 or 4 nodes.
2. Remove bottom leaves from stem with scissors to expose nodes.
3. Save the largest leaves.
4. Fill basins with approximately 1 qt. of soil.
5. Fill 4-oz. cup $^1/_2$ to $^3/_4$ full with sand and place filled cup into basin.
6. Write a label for each child.
7. Prepare activity area.

procedures
1. *Introduction:* Using the jade plant for propagation allows for easy handling by the children. Plant parts—stem, leaf, and nodes— are easily identified. The jade plant is also a useful tool to identify the color green. Find objects in the room that are green. Especially note any child's clothing that is green.
2. Have children take turns squeezing the jade plant pot.
3. Remove plant from pot.
4. Examine plant and identify root, stem, leaves.
5. Cut open a leaf and examine and identify the water inside leaf.
6. Compare potted jade with prepared cuttings (no roots).
7. Demonstrate propagation:
   a. Mix sand and soil using scoops or hands.

b. Fill 4" azalea pot with "sandy soil" and press soil to pot soil line using an empty pot of the same size.

c. Using a dibble, make a hole in the center of the pot.

d. Put jade cutting into dibble hole. Make sure that at least one node is under the soil, then press around cutting to anchor.

e. Place potted jade plant into saucer.

f. Water the plant.

g. When plant is watered, place leaf cuttings around the pot with 2"–3" of leaf petiole in soil. Make sure the top surface of the leaf is facing up.

h. Put label into pot.

8. Pass materials for propagation one item at a time and proceed one step at a time.

horticultural requirements

To propagate jade, place pots in a warm place in bright, filtered light. Water plant when top half-inch dries out. Overwatering will rot the cutting.

adaptations

One-on-one assistance may be necessary when placing leaves around the pot. This step may be skipped for some children.

hints to maximize benefits

Jades are succulents. They store water in all their fleshy parts. Don't overwater! Passing material from child to child encourages children to recognize others in the group. To help children focus, give them only the material needed to complete one step at a time.

developmental processes

· Follow one-step directions
· Practice attending skills
· Exercise tactile senses
· Reinforce strength
· Practice fine motor skills
· Practice social interaction skills

nature concepts and processes

· Plants have roots, stems, and leaves.
· Plants need water and we can see the water inside the plant.
· Some plants can grow from leaves.
· Some plants store water for another time when they need it.

vocabulary

· *sand · soil · leaves · root · stem · jade · dibble · center*

lesson 3 Propagating Kalanchoe

Horticultural concepts will be reinforced through repetition of similar activities.

materials

Soil, sand, basins or trays, 4 oz. cups, 4″ azalea pots, 4″–6″ kalanchoe cuttings; scoops, watering cans with water, saucers, permanent marker, scissors, dibbles, water.

preparation

1. Prepare kalanchoe cuttings by removing bottom leaves from stem with scissors to expose 3 or 4 nodes; remove flowers also.
2. Fill basins or trays with approximately 1 qt. of soil.
3. Fill 4-oz. cup halfway with sand and place filled cup into basin for passing.
4. Prepare activity area.

procedures

1. *Introduction:* Save the flowers removed from the kalanchoe cuttings. Brush flowers on the children's chin or arms for stimulation. Help children identify flower colors.
2. Have children take turns squeezing a potted kalanchoe plant and removing plant from pot.
3. Examine plant and identify stem, flower, leaves, roots.
4. Compare potted kalanchoe with prepared cuttings (no roots).
5. Demonstrate propagation:
   a. Incorporate sand and soil using scoops or hands.
   b. Fill 4″ azalea pot with "sandy soil" and press soil to pot soil line using an empty pot of the same size.
   c. Using a dibble, make a hole in the center of the pot.
   d. Put kalanchoe cutting into the dibble hole and press soil around cutting to anchor.
   e. Place kalanchoe pot into saucer and water gradually until water comes out the bottom.
6. Pass materials to children one item at a time and proceed one step at a time.

horticultural requirements

To propagate kalanchoe, place pots in a warm place in bright filtered light. Water plant when top half-inch dries out. Overwatering will rot the cutting. When you can see roots coming out of the bottom of the pot, kalanchoe should be placed in a sunny window.

adaptations
Children may need one-on-one assistance to complete activity.

hints to maximize benefits
Kalanchoes, like jade plants, are succulents and store water in all of their fleshy parts. Don't overwater. Passing materials from child to child and continually using their names encourages children to recognize others in the group. To help children focus, give them only the material needed to complete one step at a time.

developmental processes
· Practice following step-by-step tasks
· Reinforce recognition of others in group
· Exercise fine motor skills
· Reinforce color recognition
· Practice social and communication skills
· Exercise tactile senses

nature concepts and processes
· Plants need water.
· Plants have roots, stems, leaves, and flowers.
· Some plants need a sandy soil to grow.
· Stem cuttings have no roots.

vocabulary
· *soil* · *sand* · *root* · *stem* · *leaves* · *flowers* · *dibble* · *pot* · *scoop*
· *colors* · *center* · *kalanchoe*

lesson 4   Propagating Scented Geranium Cuttings

This lesson on stem propagation can be used as the children become more familiar with handling plants.

materials

Soil, sand, basins or trays, 4-oz. cups, 4″ pots, scented geranium plants, 4″–6″ geranium cuttings; watering cans with water, saucers, dibbles, scissors, permanent marker, labels.

preparation

1. Take cuttings from a geranium plant. Stem cuttings should be at least 4″–6″ and have at least 3 nodes.
2. Remove bottom leaves from stem to expose nodes.
3. Save the leaves.
4. Fill 4-oz. cup $\frac{1}{2}$ to $\frac{3}{4}$ full with sand and place filled cup into basin.
5. Write a label for each child.
6. Prepare activity area.

procedures

1. *Introduction:* Many varieties of scented geraniums are available in garden nurseries from late spring to early summer. Especially potent are those that have lemon and rose fragrances. You can introduce the lesson by comparing the fragrance of a rose or lemon with the oil that is released when the leaves of the scented geranium are rubbed. Remember that scented geraniums are grown for their fragrant leaves, not for their flowers.
2. Pass scented leaves to children. Encourage them to rub and smell.
3. Identify smell.
4. Compare cuttings with potted plant and identify plant parts.
5. Demonstrate propagation:
   a. Incorporate sand and soil using scoops or hands.
   b. Fill 4″ azalea pot with "sandy soil" and press soil to pot soil line using an empty pot of the same size.

   c. Using a dibble, make holes for cuttings.
   d. Put cuttings into holes, burying at least one node.

e. Firm soil around cuttings to anchor.

f. Place plant into saucer and water.

g. Put label into pot.

6. Pass materials for propagation one item at a time and proceed one step at a time.

problems

Some scented geranium stems break or bend easily. Demonstrate how to press soil firmly and carefully around stem. Have extra stem cuttings available.

adaptations

Geraniums can be propagated in a soilless mix as well. However, incorporating sand is tactually stimulating, and geraniums like a well-drained mix.

hints to maximize benefits

Rub leaves on cheeks of children, releasing fragrance. Encourage them to tickle themselves with the leaves. This stimulates the senses. The oils in the scented geranium leaves are more potent if the plant has been sitting in the sun. Have a number of scented geraniums to propagate so children can choose which smell they like the best. Have children decide if they want to plant 1, 2, or 3 stems.

developmental processes

· Practice social interaction and communication skills
· Exercise olfactory discrimination
· Exercise tactile stimulation
· Practice following sequential steps
· Reinforce fine motor skills and gentle touch
· Practice making choices

nature concepts and processes

· Identify plant parts, especially the leaves.
· Some plants' leaves are very fragrant.
· Plant leaves have a variety of textures.

vocabulary

· *geranium* · *green* · *leaves* · *smell* · *nose* · *lemon* · *rose* · *node* · *soft* · *fuzzy*

lesson 5   Collecting Pumpkin Seeds

This lesson is the cornerstone for all pumpkin seed lessons. Autumn is the best time of year for the pumpkin series.

materials
Pumpkins (variety of sizes and shapes), pumpkin-cutting knife or serrated knife, spoons or scoops for scraping out seeds, container for collecting seeds, paper towels, newspaper.

preparation
1. Prepare small pumpkins by cutting around stem but do not remove stem or top. Loosen top if necessary.
2. Set up work area by putting pumpkins of different sizes on table. Work area can be protected with newspaper.

procedures
1. *Introduction:* Put the pumpkins outdoors where it is cold. When the children are examining them, ask them how they feel. Have them touch your hands or each other's. Compare. Are we as cold or as warm as the pumpkins?
2. Have children examine, touch, feel, and smell pumpkins. Especially note color, shape, and texture. Compare sizes. Have a pumpkin that still has soil on it to show it grew on the ground.
3. Cut open larger pumpkin and have children help pull off top and reach in and pull out seeds.
4. Let each child choose a small pre-cut pumpkin and encourage them to pull off top and scoop out seeds.
5. Save some seeds to plant at a later time.

problems
For the children who do not want to touch the inside of the pumpkin, have them collect the seeds from a pumpkin top, perhaps with a soup spoon. Have paper towels available to wipe hands.

adaptations

If you do not have enough pumpkins to give one to each child, you can pair them up, each taking turns to scoop and hold the pumpkin.

hints to maximize benefits

Have different-sized scoops and spoons to accommodate the different grasps of the children. Encourage children to use hands for scooping. This activity stimulates sensory integration, encourages touching, smelling, and tasting.

developmental processes

· Stimulate tactile and olfactory senses; slippery, wet, slimy
· Exercise fine motor skills
· Compare sizes, shapes, colors, weights, textures, cold and heat
· Practice communication skills

nature concepts and processes

· Pumpkins have seeds inside.
· Pumpkins have a special smell.
· Pumpkins grow on the soil/earth.
· Pumpkins come in a variety of sizes, weights, shapes, colors, and textures.

vocabulary

· *pumpkin* · *stem* · *seed* · *orange* *scoop* · *slimy* · *shape*
· *slippery* *wet* · *round* · *circle*

lesson 6   Planting Pumpkin Seeds

This lesson will naturally follow Lesson 5, *Collecting Pumpkin Seeds*. It can be used in conjunction with Lesson 18, *Planting Citrus Seeds*.

materials

Pumpkin seeds saved from activity of collecting seeds, pumpkin; basins or trays, scoops, soil, 4″ pots, watering cans with water, saucers, labels, permanent markers, serrated knife.

preparation

For each child:

1. Place approximately 1 qt. of soil in basin.
2. Draw a line inside pot about $1/2$″ from rim of pot.
3. Write a label with child's name on one side and "pumpkin seeds" and date on other side.
4. Prepare activity area.

procedures

1. *Introduction:* Recall harvesting pumpkin seeds by opening a pumpkin and examining the seeds.
2. Demonstrate the planting of pumpkin seeds.
   a. Fill pot with soil and press firmly until soil reaches the drawn line inside pot.
   b. Place 3–5 seeds on top of soil and cover with approximately 1 inch of soil.
   c. Press soil into place.
   d. Put pot into saucer and water slowly until water comes out the bottom.
3. Pass material to children one item at a time and complete activity one step at a time as demonstrated.

problems

Children enjoy the tactile stimulation of pouring water and watching it drip from the bottom of the pot. This lesson can demonstrate the correct and incorrect way to water. Take this opportunity to show how the seeds are washed away if pot is overflowing. Explain that if the seeds are not in soil, they will not grow.

adaptations

Fill watering cans with just enough water necessary to saturate the soil.

hints to maximize benefits

Propagate pumpkin seeds about 3–4 weeks before planting activity so children can see how their planted seeds will grow or germinate. When watering, hold the pot up so children can see the drops of water coming out the bottom. This is a signal to stop watering. Encourage children to place hand under pot to feel the drops of water. This is stimulating as well as a concrete indication that watering is completed.

developmental processes
· Practice motor skills (pouring)
· Follow directions
· Reinforce memory
· Exercise tactile and olfactory senses
· Exercise eye-hand coordination

nature concepts and processes
· Seeds grow in soil.
· Seeds need water to grow.
· Water poured fast can wash away soil and seeds.

vocabulary
· *pumpkin seeds* · *orange* · *pour* · *slowly* · *fast*

lesson 7   Examining Pumpkin Seedlings

This activity is an ongoing observation experience as children examine the seedlings over a period of time.

materials
4" pots with germinated pumpkin seedlings, basins or trays.

preparation
Prepare activity area, making sure that there is a germinated pot of pumpkin seeds as well as an empty basin or tray for each child.

procedures
1. *Introduction:* Children may or may not recognize their names on the pots of seedlings. What is important is that each child recognizes the other children in the group and that they begin to recognize one another by name. By holding up the pots and identifying ownership, children begin to assimilate the knowledge that they are one of others in the group. Begin this lesson by identifying each child's pot with name (from Lesson 6, *Planting Pumpkin Seeds*) and proceed with activity.
2. Pass pots with seedlings to each child.
3. If applicable, count how many seedlings grew in each individual pot.
4. Have children squeeze pot and release soil into the basin.
5. Examine the seedlings with the children, identifying the seeds (if still in pot), roots, stem, and leaves.
6. Explain to the children that pumpkins grow outdoors when it is sunny and warm. We can grow seeds inside and we can have fun watching them grow, but we cannot grow a pumpkin indoors.

problems
Children may pull plants apart while examining seedlings. This is to be expected as they are learning. Explain that plants need all their parts to grow, again identifying leaves, stem, and roots.

adaptations

If a child cannot squeeze the pot, place the pot on its side and roll and press to release the seedlings.

hints to maximize benefits

This activity can be used in conjunction with Lesson 8, *Pumpkin Seed Picture*. Have a pot or pots of seedlings that have not been watered. Help children understand why they look different from healthy seedlings. If you have an outdoor garden, seeds can be sown directly into the ground in late spring.

developmental processes

· Exercise tactile and visual skills
· Practice communication and social skills

· Practice fine motor skills
· Reinforce name recognition
· Practice counting skills

nature concepts and processes

· Seeds grow in soil.
· Seeds grow new plants with roots, stems, and leaves.
· Pumpkins grow in soil outdoors in sun.
· All growing things need water.

vocabulary

· *pumpkin* · *seeds* · *seedlings* · *soil* · *roots* · *stem* · *leaves* · *water*

lesson 8 Creating a Pumpkin Seed Picture

This activity will be more meaningful if preceded by the previous pumpkin lessons.

materials

Pumpkin seeds, fresh pumpkin; orange construction paper, scissors, Elmer's glue, brushes for glue, small containers, knife, scoop, permanent markers.

preparation

1. Cut out pumpkin shapes from orange construction paper (round orange paper plates can be used).
2. Fill small containers with pumpkin seeds.
3. Fill small containers with glue.

procedures

1. *Introduction*: With the growing season coming to a close, start the lesson by smelling a fragrant rose or other flower from the garden. Make sure to remove any thorns before passing the rose. Put the rose in a vase of water, noting that the flower needs fresh water to stay alive for a few days.
2. Open a fresh pumpkin and identify seeds.
3. Recall previous class (collecting seeds); examine planted seedlings from previous lesson.
4. Demonstrate activity by painting construction paper pumpkin with glue and pressing seeds to glued area.
5. Show children dried seeds on pumpkin and compare to newly glued wet seeds.
6. Pass out paper pumpkins.
7. Pass out glue with brushes.
8. Apply glue to paper pumpkin.
9. Pass out seeds.
10. Press seeds into glue on pumpkin.
11. Put child's name on pumpkin and do not collect until seeds are dry.

adaptations

To decrease preparation time, use orange paper plates for the pumpkin shape. Use brown construction paper for a stem and green for leaves.

hints to maximize benefits

This activity is a good opportunity to recall previous pumpkin activities. Encourage sensory stimulation by touching, smelling, and even eating pumpkin seeds.

developmental processes

- Exercise tactile, visual, and olfactory senses
- Exercise motor skills
- Practice recall
- Compare dry and wet
- Practice step-by-step activity
- Compare colors
- Practice communication and social interaction skills
- Develop attending skills

nature concepts and processes

- Pumpkins have seeds.
- Seeds are wet inside the pumpkin.

vocabulary

- *pumpkin · seed · orange · glue · wet · dry*

lesson 9   Decorating Mini-Pumpkins

This activity can be used to reinforce horticultural concepts from previous lessons.

materials
Mini-pumpkins or gourds, floral tape, dried and preserved flowers (e.g., straw flowers, baby's breath), additional pumpkins of different sizes, permanent marker.

preparation
1. Wash soil off pumpkins and gourds and dry them. (If time permits, have the children choose their pumpkins or gourds and wash and dry them before the activity.)
2. Cut up dried material to sizes that will fit on pumpkins.
3. Fill small container with a variety of dried material.

procedures
1. *Introduction:* Bring in some fresh flowers and leaves from the garden. Especially note how soft their petals are by brushing them on the children's hands or cheeks. Compare with the dried flowers and leaves, doing the same. Have the children crush the dried leaves and ask if their hands are wet. Have them crush the fresh leaves and feel if their hands are wet.
2. Compare the large and small pumpkins, how they are alike and how they are different.
3. Demonstrate how to decorate a mini-pumpkin:
   a. Press a piece of floral tape approximately $1^1/_2''$ long onto top of pumpkin.
   b. Continue with additional tape to cover top surface.
   c. Peel paper off tape to expose sticky surface.
   d. Press flowers on tape to decorate mini-pumpkin.
4. Have each child choose a pumpkin to decorate.
5. Have children complete activity as demonstrated, one step at a time.
6. Label bottom of pumpkin with child's name.

problems
Often children may want more than one pumpkin. This presents an opportunity to talk about sharing.

adaptations
Children may need one-on-one assistance to complete this activity. When you have cut up the dried material ahead of time, it facilitates the successful completion of this activity.

hints to maximize benefits

Choose mini-pumpkins and gourds with flat tops and bottoms; it is easier to press tape onto a flat surface and dried material will sit better. When comparing large and small pumpkins, open them and compare the insides and seeds as well. Recall collecting seeds from previous lesson. Examine pumpkin seedlings.

developmental processes

· Exercise fine motor skills
· Develop tactile senses; differentiate between soft, hard, dry, wet, sticky
· Practice making choices
· Compare sizes, shapes, colors
· Compare "one" and "many"

nature concepts and processes

· Pumpkins grow to be different sizes.
· Pumpkins have seeds.
· Fresh flowers and leaves can be soft.
· Fresh leaves and flowers contain water.

vocabulary

· *big* · *little* · *orange* · *seeds* · *flowers* · *pumpkins* · *one* · *many* · *wet* · *dry* · *crush*

lesson 10   Planting Paperwhite Bulbs

This hands-on experience with planting paperwhite bulbs is a natural introduction to the lessons on tulip planting.

materials

Paperwhite bulbs, shallow containers that have no drainage holes and will accommodate 5–8 paperwhites; gravel/marble chips (marbles may be used), plastic containers to hold gravel (tray or basin will work also), scoops, watering cans with water.

preparation

1. Fill containers with gravel.
2. Ready a variety of scoops for scooping gravel.
3. Fill watering cans.
4. Prepare activity area.

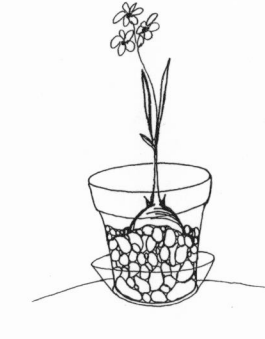

procedures

1. *Introduction:* Paperwhite flowers are sweet-smelling. Their fragrance is sensory stimulating. Force a number of paperwhites into bloom before the activity. It takes approximately 2–3 weeks for them to flower. When forcing, set the paperwhites in a clear, plastic container so the children can observe the roots, leaves, flowers, and stems. Compare the forced and unforced bulbs, encouraging the children to smell the flowers and handle the roots. Demonstrate why the rocks are needed to support the paperwhites.
2. Pass around paperwhites and identify top and bottom. Use children's bodies as examples of top (head) and bottom (feet).
3. Fill container $^2/_3$ full with gravel (have children take turns to fill).
4. Place bulbs in container (make sure children place bulbs with pointed side up).
5. Fill gravel around bulbs to secure. Leave tops exposed.
6. Add water to cover base of bulbs and put in a cool, sunny spot.
7. Check for water, especially after roots and shoots develop.

problems

Because attention spans are short and children have difficulty focusing, this group activity may be broken down into smaller groups.

adaptations

Children may have difficulty scooping up even small stones. Fill 4-oz. plastic cups with gravel weighing an amount that the children can lift successfully. Hand-over-hand may be necessary.

hints to maximize benefits

Observe the growth of the paperwhites daily with the children. If this is not possible, observe week to week. The changes are dramatic. Have each child take home a paperwhite kit to plant with adult supervision. Each kit should contain a single bulb, gravel in a sealable plastic bag, a clear plastic 4″ cup, and directions for planting (see sample note on this page).

developmental processes
· Exercise tactile, visual, and olfactory senses
· Exercise fine motor skills
· Compare bulbs to grown plants
· Follow step-by-step tasks
· Practice attending skills
· Identify top and bottom, up and down
· Practice social and communication skills
· Discriminate between heavy and light

nature concepts and processes
· The paperwhite bulb is a big container from which will grow roots, leaves, and flowers.
· Grown plants have stems, roots, leaves, and flowers.
· Bulbs and plants grow and change over time.

vocabulary
· *paperwhite* · *bulb* · *gravel* · *top* · *bottom* · *roots* · *leaves* · *flower* · *heavy* · *light*

PLANTING PAPERWHITE BULBS

Today your child has brought home a paperwhite bulb. It is ready to be forced into bloom indoors. Here's how to do it:

a. Place the bulb in the enclosed plastic cup.

b. Fill the gravel around the bulb to hold it down.

c. Fill the plastic container halfway with water.

d. Check the water level every day and add water when needed to keep the water at this level. As the bulb sprouts and grows roots, it will drink more water.

e. Place your newly planted bulb in a sunny window and it should bloom in 3 to 4 weeks.

f. Enjoy watching the bulb grow with your child. Discard the bulb and container after the flowers have died.

lesson 11   Planting Tulip Bulbs (Indoors)

Planting tulips in pots to be planted outdoors will allow the forcing of the tulips in the spring.

materials

Tulip bulbs (5 or 6 per child), container to hold tulips for children to pass, 6″ standard pots, soil, basins or trays; labels and permanent markers, scoops, saucers, watering cans with water; bunch of fresh tulips (variety of colors if possible).

preparation

1. Fill individual basins with enough soil to plant tulips.
2. Put bulbs into containers, 5 or 6 per child.
3. Write out label with variety of tulip, and date.
4. Fill watering cans.
5. With a marker, draw a line inside each pot 2 inches up from the bottom to indicate how much soil goes in before the bulbs.
6. Prepare activity area.

procedures

1. Introduce the tulip by having children touch flower, stem, and leaf. Brushing the flower on a child's cheek can be tactually stimulating.
2. Identify tulip bulbs and encourage children to handle them. Use children's bodies as examples of top (head) and bottom (feet) to help them identify the top and bottom of bulb.
3. Demonstrate planting:
   a. Fill pots with about 2″ of soil and press with an empty pot.
   b. Place bulbs in pot.
   c. Cover with soil and press to take out air pockets (hands can be used).
   d. Water and put in label.

4. Pass materials to children one item at a time and proceed one step at a time as demonstrated.

5. Save potted tulips for planting outdoors another time.

problems

Some children may not understand the concept of pointing up and down. Place bulbs on tray the way they are to be planted and emphasize the proper way to plant as the children do the activity.

adaptations

The 6″ pots may be difficult for some children to fill. One-on-one assistance may be required with some, and hand-over-hand may be necessary to complete the task.

hints to maximize benefits

Drawing the line may help children fill the pot correctly. Although fresh tulips may be difficult to obtain, having fresh tulip flowers helps to make a concrete, tactile connection between bulb and flower.

developmental processes

· Practice attending to task
· Exercise motor skills
· Follow step-by-step directions
· Practice up/down, top/bottom
· Practice communication and social interaction skills
· Practice color discrimination

nature concepts and processes

· Tulip plants grow from bulbs.
· Tulip bulbs have tops and bottoms.
· Bulbs need to be planted right-side-up.
· A tulip plant has roots, stem, leaves, and flower.
· Some flowers have different colors.
· Some flowers smell.

vocabulary

· *tulip · bulb · colors of tulips · top · bottom · up · soil*

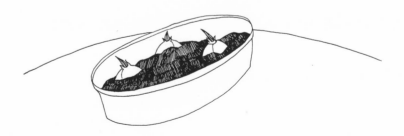

lesson 12   Planting Tulip Bulbs (Outdoors)

This activity is seasonal. Tulips need a cold spell to flower. They are usually planted outdoors in the autumn.

materials
Potted tulip bulbs from last session; trowel or shovel to dig holes, scoops or shovels for children, watering cans with water; fresh tulips, bulbs.

preparation
1. Set up planting stations in outdoor garden.
2. Dig holes, as many as you need, to sink pots (rim of pot should also be covered with soil).
3. Set tulip pots (with labels) next to hole.
4. Place shovel or scoop with pot.
5. Fill watering cans with water.

procedures
1. *Introduction:* Planting in the garden provides an opportunity for the children to "dig in the dirt" and observe the garden at different times of the year. In autumn the leaves are different colors and some may have fallen on the ground. What are the colors they see?
2. Recall last week's activity with fresh tulips, bulbs, and pots with label.
3. Demonstrate the planting activity by placing pot in ground, covering pot with soil (label should be visible).
4. Water.
5. Have children choose a station to plant and complete activity.

problems

Physical disabilities may not allow some children to plant from wheelchairs. The activity may be adapted by planting in raised beds or by preparing the activity area with a blanket for a child to sit or lie on while planting.

adaptations

Most children will need one-on-one assistance to complete task.

hints to maximize benefits

Encourage exploration in the garden. Encourage children to water other plants in the garden. Have a handy water supply or extra watering cans available. Have small rakes handy to help children gather leaves.

developmental processes

· Exercise fine and gross motor skills
· Exercise visual discriminating skills
· Practice communication and social interaction skills
· Explore the earth and soil

nature concepts and processes

· Plants grow in soil in the ground.
· Plants need water to grow.

· Gardens change with the seasons.
· Temperature changes with the seasons.
· Leaves turn colors and fall to the ground in autumn.

vocabulary

· tulip · bulb · soil · colors · earth
· pot · label · leaves · autumn

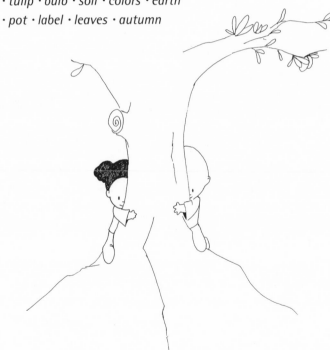

lesson 13   Recipe for Good Earth

It is never too early to learn about taking care of our world.

materials

Brown fallen leaves (dry), fresh green clippings (grass); scoops, plastic container with lid (at least shoe-box size), pick or drill ($1/8''$ bit) to puncture container, small spray bottles with water; permanent marker, heavy construction paper, basin with garden soil; tape or masking tape.

preparation

1. Puncture the sides, top, and bottom of the empty plastic container.
2. Collect dry brown leaves and place in basin. (If possible, have the children collect the leaves.)
3. Collect green plant material (grass clippings) and place in basin.
4. Fill small spray bottles with water.
5. Design COMPOST sign.
6. Prepare work area.

procedures

1. *Introduction:* Children often participate in preparing food for a family meal. Build upon this experience. Introduce this compost lesson by mingling ingredients used in baking in a large bowl (for example, flour, milk, salt, water, sugar). Each child can add a different ingredient. (Most children want to add the eggs. Be prepared with an ample supply.) Have them take turns adding ingredients and mixing. Equate activity to recipe for good earth. Dispose of bowl with baking ingredients before continuing. (Do not add to compost.)
2. Pass basin of rich garden soil and encourage children to describe how it feels.
3. Explain that soil is made from leaves and plants, grass, veggies, peels, orange skins, onions, and so forth.
4. Make a compost bin with children:
   a. Have children examine the bin and note the holes in it. Put a piece of paper inside and blow through the holes, noting how the paper moves.
   b. Pass brown dry leaves to children and have them crumple the leaves with their hands.
   c. Layer the bin with crumpled leaves.
   d. Pass the green plant materials to children and discuss what is in the material and sprinkle over top of brown leaves.

e. Continue layering, with a layer of leaves (approximately 2"–3") followed by a thin layer of green plant material (approximately 2").

f. When children have completed layering, have them spray some water into the compost bin, taking turns with the spray bottle.

g. Place the top on the bin and have the children press it down.

h. Label with the COMPOST sign.

i. Twice a month, examine the contents with the children and turn it by dumping into a container of the same size. Check for moisture and add if necessary.

j. Save the good earth for future use in planting.

problems

Children may have difficulty waiting for bin to be filled. Choose a bin that can be filled in a timely fashion with the children.

adaptations

You can scoop green plant material into the bin. If that is difficult, put green plant material into a 4-oz. cup for children to sprinkle into the bin.

hints to maximize benefits

Making compost is an activity that is timely in the spring, when you are cleaning up the garden as it is awakening, and the autumn when preparing the garden for going to sleep. Composting can be an ongoing activity. If you have garden worms, place them on top of layered compost so children can examine. Explain that animals such as worms live in the soil and help make good earth. (If you followed the introduction, mixing baking ingredients using eggs, then be sure to use the crushed eggshells in the good earth mix.)

developmental processes

· Exercise tactile and olfactory senses
· Practice fine motor skills
· Reinforce sequencing skills
· Practice social skills
· Develop communication skills

nature concepts and processes

· Green plants and brown leaves make soil.
· Soil can be made like a recipe for food.
· Worms live in good earth.
· Grass and leaves smell different.
· Nature recycles its used-up stuff.

vocabulary

· *soil* · *air* · *leaves* · *grass* · *worms* · *earth* · *recipe* · *layers* · *compost* · *recycle*

lesson 14   Planting Potatoes

Potato eyes are fast growers and fun to watch daily.

materials
Potatoes with eyes, soil, pots, basins or trays; knife, scoops, watering cans with water; assortment of potatoes for comparison, e.g., red, baking, sweet potatoes.

preparation
1. Fill basins or trays with approximately 1 qt. of soil.
2. Write each child's name with marker on pot.
3. Prepare activity area.

procedures
1. *Introduction:* Place individual potatoes into pots of soil and encourage the children to "dig" for the potatoes. Have different varieties in each pot and have children compare for similarities and differences.
2. Discuss the appearance of the potatoes.
3. Identify the eyes of the potatoes and discuss differences between our eyes and the eyes of the potatoes. Put glasses on a potato and ask if potatoes wear glasses. Who wears glasses in the group? People see better with glasses but potatoes do not see. What are their eyes for?

4. Collect whole potatoes and demonstrate planting activity:
   a. Cut up potato into pieces, making sure there are eyes on each piece.
   b. Fill pot $\frac{1}{3}$ full with soil and place potato piece in pot (flat side touching soil).
   c. Cover potato with soil, pressing it around cutting.
   d. Place potted potato in saucer, and water.
5. Pass materials to children one item at a time and proceed one step at a time.

problems

If you use this activity many weeks into the curriculum, the children will be used to handling the planting medium (soil). If you use it too early in the sequence, some children might not want to handle the soil.

adaptations

One-on-one assistance may be necessary for those children who are physically unable to complete the activity.

hints to maximize benefits

Grow a potato plant ahead of time so children can take apart the plant and examine plant parts. Have foods that we get from potatoes available for children to taste. This can be the conclusion of the activity.

developmental processes

· Follow step-by-step directions
· Reinforce recognition of others
· Exercise olfactory, tactile, visual, and taste sensations
· Compare human eyes and potato eyes
· Practice communication and social interaction skills

nature concepts and processes

· Potatoes have eyes that can grow.
· A potato, like a bulb, is a swollen root that stores food and water for a plant.

vocabulary

· *potato* · *eyes* · *soil* · *water* · *glasses*

lesson 15   Planting Carrot Tops

Using kitchen scraps can be fun.

materials
Fresh carrots with greens, carrot seeds in package, soil, 4″ azalea pots; watering cans with water, scoops, labels, permanent markers, scissors, knife for cutting carrots, basins or trays, plastic knives that children can use.

preparation
For each child:

1. Write name on label with marker.
2. Fill basin or tray with approximately 1 qt. of soil.
3. Cut off approximately 1″ of carrot tops with greens.
4. Trim greens to about 4″. Save one carrot for each child to prepare.
5. Prepare 3 carrots for each child. You can also do this as a group project for the classroom using one carrot per child.
6. Draw line inside pot approximately 2″ below rim with marker.
7. Prepare activity area.

procedures
1. *Introduction:* This activity goes hand-in-hand with *Recipe for Good Earth* (Lesson 13). Have the children slice off the top greens from the carrot and cut them into small pieces. Add them to the compost bin and have them take turns turning. Note the changes of the compost from when they first made the recipe.
2. Talk about carrots (color, shape, taste). Explain that carrots can grow only from seed, but that the carrot tops, if planted with a bit of the carrot still attached, will stay alive and grow.
3. Open the seed package and examine the seeds.
4. It is also fun to plant the tops to identify the parts of plant as they grow.
5. Demonstrate activity:
   a. Take whole carrot with leaves and cut approximately 1″ off carrot top.
   b. Trim greens to about 4″.
   c. Fill pot with soil and press with empty pot so top of soil is about 2″ below top rim of pot.
   d. Place 3 prepared carrot tops into pot, carrot piece down, and cover with soil.
   e. Water.
   f. Label with name.
5. Pass materials to children one item at a time and proceed one step at a time.
6. Enjoy carrot sticks with children when activity is complete.

adaptations

Carrot tops will also grow in water and can be secured in the containers with small pebbles.

hints to maximize benefits

Plant a couple of carrot tops about 3 weeks before activity so children will see completed project. This activity provides the opportunity for children to work with something that is familiar to them. If you have access to an outdoor garden, plant the carrot seeds outdoors. Follow the package directions. If you planted tulips in the garden in the fall, identify the growing tulips to the children when they are planting the carrot seeds.

developmental processes

- Stimulate taste, tactile, and olfactory senses
- Practice fine motor skills
- Develop strength for cutting activities
- Identify colors, shapes, and plant parts
- Practice social skills

nature concepts and processes

- Carrots are orange.
- Carrots grow from seed.
- Carrot tops can be planted and will grow roots.
- Carrot plants have roots and leaves.
- Leaves have different shapes and smells.
- Carrots, which we eat, grow underground.
- Green discards from garden are good for compost.

vocabulary

- *carrot* · *orange* · *compost*

lesson 16 Planting an Avocado Pit

Tasting avocado meat may be a new experience.

materials
Avocado pit, washed of fruit, 4" standard pot, soil, basins or trays, scoops, labels, permanent marker, knife, clear wrap.

preparation
For each child:
1. Prepare pit for planting by removing fruit and washing pit.
2. Fill basin or tray with 1 qt. of soil.
3. Write name on label with marker.
4. Draw halfway line inside pot with marker.

procedures
1. *Introduction:* Avocado is a fruit that is enjoyed in many cultures, and recipes for using avocado abound. Save the fruit from the avocado and prepare a snack with the children. Following your favorite simple recipe for avocado dip, have the children take turns adding the ingredients and mixing. This is a "tasty" introduction to the lesson of propagating an avocado plant from a seed.
2. Identify avocado.
3. Cut out slices and pass.
4. Have children taste and feel.
5. Teach children that this pit is a seed.
6. Identify larger (basal) end of seed as the part that sits in the soil.
7. Demonstrate how to plant:
   a. Fill pot halfway with soil and press to firm soil to line drawn inside pot.
   b. Place avocado seed with large, flat side touching soil.
   c. Fill soil around seed, pressing in place and leaving top third of seed exposed.
   d. Water.
   e. Put label into side of pot, making sure not to damage seed.
   f. Cover with clear plastic wrap.
8. Pass materials to children one item at a time and complete activity one step at a time.

problems
Some children may not like the texture of the avocado meat (it is oily). Encourage them to feel the skin instead. Also make sure that the children have placed the basal end of the seed into the pot.

horticultural requirements
Avocados are rewarding plants to grow indoors—they will grow very tall and wide. They need lots of sun. Water them thoroughly at least

once a week, more often if the room is very hot, dry, and/or sunny. If they are growing well, they can be transplanted into larger pots every six months.

hints to maximize benefits
The large Florida avocado has medium-green, glossy skin and is easily germinated. Use ripe avocados. Have each child harvest seed from a ripe avocado and wash to prepare for planting. Compare avocado seed with smaller seeds.

developmental processes
· Practice sequencing (step-by-step) as in recipes
· Reinforce social skills
· Stimulate olfactory, taste, and tactile senses

nature concepts and processes
· Some seeds are very big.
· Fruits are soft and edible, while the seeds are hard.
· Plants can be propagated from large seeds as well as from small seeds.

vocabulary
· *avocado* · *seed* · *green* · *big* · *large* · *small* · *hard* · *soft*

lesson 17   Collecting Citrus Seeds

Harvesting seeds from citrus will continue to build the children's knowledge of plant parts.

materials

Oranges, grapefruits, and lemons with seeds; serrated knife, paper plates, paper towels, plastic container for collecting seeds; plastic juicer with jar for squeezing juice.

preparation

1. Wash and dry citrus fruits.
2. Prepare area for activity.

procedures

1. *Introduction:* Citrus fruits are part of the diet of most children. This lesson will allow you to build on that knowledge.
2. Roll uncut fruit one at a time to each child after identifying fruit and color.
3. Encourage children to pass to one another and continue by making comparisons (big/little, large/small).
4. Have children pass fruit back to teacher.
5. Cut open the citrus fruits one at a time and observe what is inside the fruit; identify seeds.
6. Squeeze the fruit and note that the fruit also has juice.

7. If possible, set a hand juicer on top of a jar. Let children help squeeze the juice.
8. Give each child a cut-open fruit and have them harvest the seeds to save for the planting activity.
9. Encourage children to taste fruit after harvesting seeds. (Have slices ready to serve that have not been handled by the group.)

problems
Most children are familiar with fruit and anticipate tasting. However, it is important to know if any of the children cannot eat citrus fruit.

hints to maximize benefits
If possible, buy "Ponderosa" lemons from Florida (available at the end of January). They are huge, and comparisons to small lemons can be made. The sour taste of lemons is quite stimulating. Have empty cartons of citrus juices and encourage children to pair cartons with fruit.

developmental processes
· Exercise motor skills
· Exercise olfactory, tactile, visual, and taste senses
· Compare large/small, colors
· Practice communication skills; names
· Reinforce social skills; sharing; recognition

nature concepts and processes
· We eat fruit.
· Fruit has seeds and juice.
· Fruits are different—sizes, colors, tastes.
· Lemons are sour.
· Citrus can be sour or sweet.

vocabulary
· *orange* · *grapefruit* · *lemon* · *seeds* · *colors* · *juice* · *sour* · *sweet* · *squeeze*

lesson 18   Planting Citrus Seeds

Waiting for seeds to germinate requires patience.

materials
Seeds collected from previous lesson, soil, basins or trays, scoops, 4″ pots, watering cans with water, permanent marker, clear plastic wrap.

preparation
1. Fill basins or trays with approximately 1 qt. of soil.
2. Write each child's name on a pot.
3. Fill watering cans.
4. Draw inside pot with magic marker about 1½″ from rim of pot to indicate soil level.
5. Prepare activity area.

procedures
1. *Introduction:* This lesson, if followed in sequence, will be the second time that children will be planting harvested seeds. (See Lesson 6, *Planting Pumpkin Seeds.*) Citrus seeds take much longer to germinate than pumpkin seeds. Plant citrus seeds about 8 weeks prior to this activity in anticipation of maximizing the learning potential of this lesson. Use the propagated seedlings to examine the roots, stems, and leaves, and often the seeds as well, if they are still attached.

2. Recall collecting seeds by opening citrus fruit and looking for seeds.
3. Demonstrate planting:
   a. Fill pot with soil to line drawn inside pot and compact soil with additional empty pot.
   b. Place seeds on compacted soil and cover with additional soil.
   c. Water pot.
   d. Place a piece of clear wrap on top to keep in moisture.
4. Pass material for planting to children and encourage them to follow planting directions one step at a time.
5. Put pots under lights in cart or place on a sunny windowsill. Examine every week.

problems

If tasting will be part of this lesson, it is important to know if any of the children cannot eat citrus fruit.

adaptations

If children have difficulty picking up seeds, put them into plastic tubes (such as the water picks used to keep flower stems in water). It is easier for children to grasp tubes and spread seeds.

hints to maximize benefits

It takes about 5–6 weeks for seeds to germinate. Bottom heat encourages germination. Compare pumpkin seeds to citrus seeds. Plant pumpkin seeds at the same time as the citrus seeds and compare the germination time.

developmental processes

· Practice recall
· Exercise fine motor skills
· Follow step-by-step tasks
· Practice sequencing of steps

nature concepts and processes

· Seeds grow in soil.
· Seeds can come from fruit.
· Seeds are hard for protection.
· Seeds grow whole new plants with roots, stems, and leaves.

vocabulary

· *seeds* · *lemon* · *grapefruit* · *orange* · *colors* · *soil* · *hard*

lesson 19   Transplanting Citrus Seedlings

Transplanted seedlings are slow growers.

materials

Propagated citrus seedlings, soil, scoops, basins or trays, 4" azalea pots, dibbles, saucers, watering cans with water.

preparation

1. Fill basins or trays with approximately 1 qt. of soil.
2. Write an identification label for each child.
3. Fill watering cans.
4. Prepare activity area.

procedures

1. *Introduction:* This is the first transplanting activity for the children. To help the children understand how to handle the seedlings properly, pass around an egg. It can be hard boiled or uncooked. Note what occurs as they hand it to one another. Equate this to handling seedlings. Encourage gentle/soft touch.
2. Recall previous lesson by presenting children with citrus, cutting it open, and identifying seeds.
3. Identify stem, leaves, roots.
4. Compare with seed.
5. Demonstrate how to transplant seedling:
   a. Fill 4" pot with soil and press soil to line using an empty pot of the same size.
   b. Make a big dibble hole in the middle of the pot.
   c. Plant seedling, making sure root is in the soil.
   d. Place transplanted pot in saucer, and water.
6. Pass materials to children one item at a time and proceed one step at a time.
7. Place seedlings under lights in cart or place on a sunny windowsill.

problems

Children may pull plant apart when examining seedlings; have extras on hand to ensure success.

adaptations

If it is not feasible to grow citrus seedlings, a transplanting lesson can be taught using pumpkin seedlings grown from seeds collected in the fall.

hints to maximize benefits

Bottom heat encourages germination of the seedlings. Because the citrus seeds take a long time to germinate, plant them in individual cells about 2 months prior to this activity. Each cell will contain a seedling for the children to transplant.

developmental processes

- Exercise fine motor skills
- Practice a gentle/soft touch
- Reinforce understanding of opposites
- Practice social and communication skills
- Reinforce name recognition of others
- Reinforce sequencing

nature concepts and processes

- Plants grow from seeds.
- Some seeds grow faster than others.
- Plants need to be treated gently.
- We know a plant or a seed is alive because it grows and changes.
- Plants have roots, stems, and leaves.

vocabulary

· *seed* · *seedlings* · *root* · *stem* · *leaves* · *soil* · *gentle* · *soft* · *touch*

lesson 20   Propagation by Division

The root development of a plant is an important part of this lesson.

materials
Chinese evergreen plants, basins or trays, scoops, 4″ or 5″ standard pots, watering cans with water, saucers, labels, permanent markers, soil.

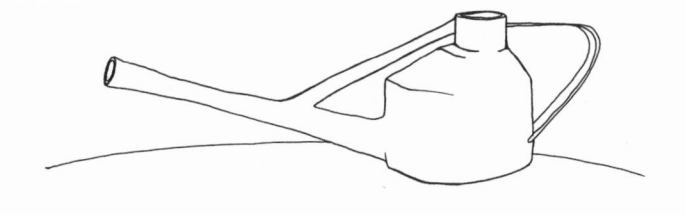

preparation
1. Buy Chinese evergreen plants in 6″ pots.
2. Fill basins or trays with 1–1½ qt. of soil (depending on size of plants to be divided).
3. Make sure you have correct pot size for division. 4″ and 5″ standard pots should suffice.
4. Fill watering cans.
5. Make a label with child's name and the name of the plant.
6. Draw a line inside pot with marker indicating approximately ½″ of soil.
7. Prepare activity area.

procedures
1. *Introduction:* If space allows, put children close together within a circle, with a string or chalk around the circle. Pretend they are planted in a pot. Explain how crowded it is when they are close together. Squeeze each child's hand gently as if they were planted and needed to be loosened. Take each child to the work area one at a time. Compare this activity to the division of a plant.
2. Pass pot with plants around to children, having them squeeze pot to release plants.
3. Remove plants from container.
4. Examine and identify plant parts, especially the roots.
5. Have children divide plant, each receiving one plant with roots intact.
6. Do planting activity with children:
   a. Fill pot to marker line and press with empty pot.
   b. Tuck roots into pot and fill with soil, leaving crown exposed.
   c. Firm soil around plant.
   d. Place plant into saucer.

e. Water until water comes out the bottom.
f. Label.

problems

Children may have problems tucking in the roots and leaving the crown of the plant uncovered. One-on-one assistance is recommended.

hints to maximize benefits

This activity is a good lesson to identify the plant parts, roots, and leaves. It is an activity that can be meaningful any time of year. It is important to know the horticultural requirements of these plants. Chinese evergreens do not like direct sunlight and do well in low-light locations. Don't let them dry out.

developmental processes

· Practice taking turns
· Practice squeezing as a motor skill
· Identify parts of plants
· Reinforce social and communication skills

nature concepts and processes

· Plants need water to live.
· Plants have roots, stems, and leaves.
· Plants can be propagated by dividing or separating them.

vocabulary

· *Chinese evergreen* · *evergreen* · *division* · *squeeze*
· *divide/separate*

lesson 21 Aloe Vera Propagation

Plants are grown and used for medicine.

materials
Aloe plants to be divided, soil, sand, dibbles, basins or trays, scoops, watering cans with water, saucers, permanent marker, 4″ azalea or 4″ standard pots, 4-oz. cups, store-bought products containing aloe.

preparation
1. Fill basin or tray with approximately 1 qt. of soil.
2. Fill 4-oz. cups ½ to ¾ full with sand.
3. Place cup of sand in basin.
4. Write each child's name with marker on pot.
5. Prepare activity area.

procedures
1. *Introduction:* Children are beginning to learn that plants give us food. Dividing an aloe plant for propagation is an excellent opportunity to teach the children that some plants are used for medicine. Bring in products that contain aloe, such as suntan lotion, shampoo, lip balm, lipstick, etc. Help the children identify the products. Explain that aloe is one of the ingredients in the prod-

ucts and describe how they are used. Ask the children what part of the plant is used and proceed with the lesson.
2. Cut open aloe leaf and pass around, encouraging children to feel and smell.
3. Have children take turns squeezing pot to release aloe plants.
4. Identify plant parts (leaves and roots).
5. Demonstrate propagation of aloe:
   a. Pour sand into soil and incorporate, using scoops or hands.
   b. Fill pot with "sandy soil" and pack with empty pot.
   c. Make dibble hole in middle of pot large enough for roots to fit into.
   d. Plant aloe and firm soil around roots.
   e. Put plant in saucer, and water.

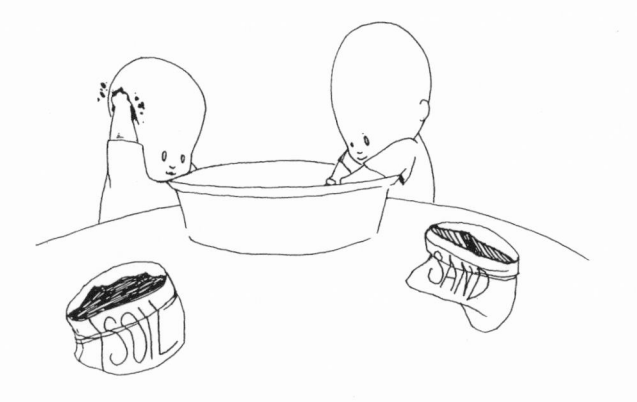

problems

Children are beginning to anticipate steps in propagation sequence and are working more independently. However, one-on-one assistance may be necessary for some children to successfully complete the activity.

adaptations

This is a relatively simple activity with no adaptation except for those children with individual special needs.

hints to maximize benefits

Banana Boat makes an aloe vera gel in a pump bottle. It is green (same as aloe) and the pump is easy for most children to use. When children have completed the propagation and washed their hands, pass around the aloe vera gel to rub on clean hands.

developmental processes

· Follow step-by-step directions
· Utilize motor skills
· Practice waiting turns
· Practice communication skills
· Reinforce name recognition of others
· Reinforce sharing and social skills

nature concepts and processes

· We can make medicine and other products from plants.
· Plants can be propagated by division.
· Some plants are best grown in a sandy soil mixture.
· Some types of plants store water in their leaves.

vocabulary

· *green* · *aloe* · *roots* · *leaves* · *medicine*

lesson 22   Spider Plant Propagation

The comparison of spider plants to the garden or household spider is very obvious.

materials

Large mother spider plant, basins or trays, scoops, soil, 4" pots, watering cans with water; saucers, labels, permanent markers, dibbles; coated floral wire to anchor plant, rubber spider.

preparation

1. Collect live spiders and put in jar with holes at the top.
2. If possible, hang plant for children to see.
3. Fill each basin with approximately 1 qt. of soil.
4. Fill watering cans with water.
5. Write label with name of plant, child's name, and date.
6. Propagate spider plant for demonstration.
7. Cut wire into approximately 5" lengths and bend into a "U" shape.

procedures

1. *Introduction:* Autumn and spring are good times to find spiders in the house and garden. Collect spiders and place them in a jar. Encourage the children to look at the spiders in the jar. Compare the shapes of the spiders with the spider plant. If live spiders are not readily available, use a rubber one. Note the legs of the spider and the roots of the plant. (Release the spiders after the activity.)
2. Talk about the spider plant and compare with a live or rubberized spider.

3. Cut off baby spider plants growing on long stems of the mother plant and have children identify roots and leaves.
4. Demonstrate propagation:
   a. Fill pot with soil to line and press firmly to compact soil.
   b. Make a hole with the dibble large enough to accommodate the roots of the baby spider plants and place plant roots into the hole.
   c. Press soil around plant to anchor.
   d. Put spider plant pot into saucer.
   e. Water.
   f. Label.
   g. If necessary, anchor plant into soil by bending a wire in half in the shape of a "U" and placing it over the crown of the plant. (This can be removed once the plant is established.)
5. Pass materials to children one item at a time and proceed one step at a time.

problems

If you use the wire to anchor the plants, make sure it is coated to minimize rust. If a plant is not taken home immediately, you can remove wire after roots are established. You do not need the wire anchor to have a successful planting.

horticultural requirements

Spider plants are easy to propagate but will not look good if they get too much light or if they are allowed to dry out. They like high humidity and bright, filtered light. Water weekly.

hints to maximize benefits

Have children choose a plant to be propagated from the mother plant. Encourage children to plant more than one if they have the interest, and their attention span allows them to focus.

developmental processes

· Practice fine motor skills
· Compare shapes, forms, and colors
· Follow directions
· Practice communication skills

nature concepts and processes

· Plants need roots to grow.
· Some plants can grow in the air.

vocabulary

· *spider plant* · *root* · *spider*

lesson 23   Pothos Propagation

This lesson can be used any time of year.

materials

Pothos plant, basins or trays, scoops, soil, 4″ pots, watering cans with water, saucers, labels, permanent markers, dibbles.

preparation

1. Fill basins or trays with approximately 1 qt. of soil.
2. Prepare pothos cuttings by cutting from mother plant, leaving at least one inch on either side of node, which will produce roots.
3. Fill watering cans with water.
4. Write label with child's name, date, and name of plant.
5. Propagate pothos for demonstration.

procedures

1. *Introduction:* If you use this activity toward the end of the curriculum, you might want to plant the pothos cutting upside down and have the children tell you what you are doing wrong. Encourage the children to "teach" you the right way to plant.
2. Pass around single node cuttings and encourage children to feel bud of root.
3. Explain that the root must be in the soil to grow.
4. Demonstrate propagation activity:
    a. Fill pot with soil to line and press firmly to compact soil.
    b. Make a hole with a dibble and place cutting into hole with top of leaf showing. (Note that the node is under the soil.)
    c. Continue until pot is full (5–7 cuttings).
    d. Firm soil around each cutting.
    e. Place pot in saucer.
    f. Water.
    g. Label.
5. Pass materials to children one item at a time and proceed one step at a time.

problems

Some children may have trouble with multi-steps of making dibble hole and putting stem into hole. Sturdy stems can be pushed directly into soil, skipping the dibbling step if necessary. One-on-one attention is recommended. For safety, cut the pothos ahead of time and do not give children scissors.

adaptations
Some children may have the attention span to place only one cutting into the soil. This is a successful propagation.

horticultural requirements
Remember that pothos is a low-light plant and does not like direct sunlight. Keep soil evenly moist; water weekly.

hints to maximize benefits
Until this lesson, children have basically handled one-stem propagation and transplanting. This activity should be done after children are used to the materials and are familiar with planting. Select a pothos plant that is mature with sturdy stems for children to handle.

developmental processes
- Practice attending to task
- Practice following multi-step directions
- Reinforce fine motor skills

nature concepts and processes
- Plants need roots to grow.
- Plants can be grown (propagated) from a single leaf and node piece.
- Plants have leaves, stems, and roots.
- Nodes are the growing points of plants.
- Roots will grow from nodes on stems.

vocabulary
- *pothos* · *node* · *under* · *root* · *grow/propagate* · *single*

lesson 24   Collecting Sunflower Seeds

This lesson demonstrates that flowers produce seeds.

materials
Dried sunflower heads saved from the autumn, fresh sunflowers from a florist; small plastic containers to collect seeds, trays to place sunflower heads on, vase with water for fresh sunflowers; packaged shelled sunflower seeds for tasting, if appropriate.

preparation
1. Place dried sunflower heads on trays.
2. Fill vase with water and fresh sunflowers.
3. Prepare activity area.

procedures
1. *Introduction:* By the time you are ready to begin the unit on sunflowers, the citrus seeds planted in the winter should be germinated. Examine the seedlings with the children, noting how slowly they are growing. Choose a germinated seedling that still has the seed attached to the root of the new plant. Squeeze the pot to release the citrus plant and examine the roots, stem, leaves, and seed. Since the sunflowers grow much faster than the citrus, you can examine the plants on a weekly basis to note the differences.

2. Present dried sunflower heads and have children examine and harvest seeds.
3. Compare live sunflowers with dried sunflowers, especially noting that the live flower is kept fresh in water, has green leaves and stem and probably has not produced seeds.
4. Collect seeds for planting from the dried heads.
5. Open dried seed shell and examine meat.
6. Taste sunflower seeds that have been commercially prepared, if appropriate.
7. Have children place live sunflowers in a vase to enjoy in room.

problems

Seeds can be sharp and some children may have problems with fine motor skills when harvesting. You might have to loosen seeds from the dried sunflower head for some children.

hints to maximize benefits

Separate the shells from the seeds ahead of time so children can examine them easily. Have dried sunflower heads of different sizes so children can make comparisons (big/little).

developmental processes

· Stimulate tactile sensation and fine motor skills
· Stimulate visual exploration
· Practice communication skills
· Explore opposites
· Compare sizes

nature concepts and processes

· Plants have different parts.
· Sunflowers have seeds in flower heads.
· We can eat many seeds.
· Different plants have different seeds.
· Dry seeds are different from wet or fresh seeds.

vocabulary

· *sunflower* · *seed* · *stem* · *leaves* · *roots* · *big* · *little* · *wet* · *dry* · *vase* · *petals*

lesson 25 Planting Sunflower Seeds

This lesson will build upon previous lessons. Sunflower seeds germinate quickly.

materials

Dried sunflower heads, sunflower seeds harvested from last week, soil; basins or trays, scoops, watering cans with water, saucers, labels, permanent marker, 4" pots; shelled seeds for tasting.

preparation

For each child:

1. Place approximately 1 qt. of soil in basin or tray.
2. Draw a line inside pot about $1/2$" from rim of pot.
3. Write a label with each child's name and name of sunflower variety if known.
4. Prepare activity area.

procedures

1. *Introduction:* Children will learn by repetition. Once again, bring in a fresh sunflower. Rub the petals of the flowers on the cheeks, hands, or arms of the children and have them identify the name of the flower. If they cannot recall the name, compare the sunflower to the yellow sun in the sky. If fresh sunflowers were not part of your introductory lesson, they can be used to introduce any of the sunflower lessons.
2. Recall harvesting sunflower seeds from last lesson by examining a sunflower head.
3. Demonstrate propagation of seeds:
   a. Fill pot with soil and press firmly until soil reaches line inside pot.
   b. Place seeds on top of soil and cover with approximately 1" of soil.
   c. Press soil in place and put pot in saucer, and water.
   d. Put label in pot on the side.
4. Pass materials to children one item at a time and complete activity one step at a time.

problems

Children may want to eat seeds with shells as they recall last week's activity. Remind them that these seeds are for planting. They can have shelled seeds for tasting when activity is completed.

hints to maximize benefits

There are dwarf varieties of sunflowers. They include "Music Box," "Teddy Bear," "Sunset," and "Sunspot." These can be bought in many garden centers in the spring as well as through catalogues such as the

Burpee Seed Company's. When you plant any seeds, it is important to label clearly the variety planted and the date. Start sunflower seedlings about one month prior to activity so children can examine germinated seedlings. Especially identify roots and shoots.

developmental processes
· Practice recall
· Reinforce sensory-motor skills
· Practice sequencing

nature concepts and processes
· Sunflowers have seeds.
· Seeds need soil and water to grow.
· Sunflowers come in many different sizes and colors.

vocabulary
· *sunflower seeds* · *colors*

lesson 26 Transplanting Sunflower Seedlings

Children will be able to watch their seedlings grow to maturity.

materials

Propagated sunflower seedlings (a mini-variety such as "Music Box," "Teddy Bear," "Sunset," or "Sunspot") in cell packs, soil; basins, scoops, small trowels or shovels for digging a hole (dibbles may also be used), watering cans with water, permanent marker; containers for transplanted seedlings, such as window boxes or large standing containers.

preparation

1. Move containers to a location where they will be accessible to the children.
2. Set up planting stations.
3. Fill basins with soil.
4. Place propagated plants near stations.

5. With permanent marker, write labels with children's names as well as variety of sunflower.
6. Draw line in container with permanent marker to indicate soil line.
7. Fill watering cans with water.

procedures

1. *Introduction:* If you planted potted tulip bulbs outdoors in the autumn, dig up one of the pots and have the children examine. Squeeze the pot with the children to release the plants. If the tulips are late-blooming, they may have the flower as well as the roots, stem, and leaves intact. Explain that the sunflower seedlings will grow flowers when it is hot and the tulips will no longer be flowering.
2. Demonstrate transplanting:
   a. Fill container to soil line; leave soil loose.
   b. Dig a hole large enough to hold seedling.
   c. Pop seedling out of cell pack, holding firmly by the root ball.
   d. Drop seedling into hole.
   e. Firm soil around seedling; be sure not to bury the stem.
   f. Water.
   g. Label.

3. With one-on-one assistance, have children transplant seedlings as demonstrated.

problems

Planters can be very large and require a quantity of soil that children cannot handle. Fill planters ahead of time, leaving enough soil for children to complete the filling task. Make sure you have gently firmed the soil before children proceed with the activity. They might take it out of the container rather than putting it in if it's too loose. Ideally, sunflower seedlings can be planted directly into the ground if you have access to an outdoor garden.

adaptations

If you have not been able to start sunflower seedlings indoors but you would still like to have a sunflower garden, you can purchase plants at your local nursery. Make sure to read the planting label to know how tall the plants will be. The seeds can also be planted directly into the soil. Follow planting directions on the package.

hints to maximize benefits

Make sure that each workstation is accessible. Sunflowers can also be planted in raised beds or directly into the ground in a flower bed.

developmental processes

· Exercise sensorimotor stimulation
· Practice fine and gross motor skills
· Practice standing balance
· Follow directions
· Practice social skills

nature concepts and processes

· Sunflowers grow outdoors. They need to be planted in the soil.
· Sunflowers need sun (heat and light) and water to grow.
· Tulip plant and sunflower seedling differ in size, shape.

vocabulary

· *seedlings · stem · leaves · sunflowers · roots · soil · tulip*
· *flowers · hot · summer · sun · heat*

lesson 27   Making Sunflower Seed Pictures

This lesson will be more meaningful if preceded by the previous sunflower lessons.

materials

Sunflower seeds, white construction paper with outlined picture of a sunflower, yellow construction paper, Elmer's glue or glue sticks, brushes for glue, permanent markers, small containers for seeds, scissors, Styrofoam or plastic containers for glue.

preparation

1. Draw outlined picture of sunflower and have it copied for each child.
2. Cut out yellow petals of sunflower.
3. Fill small containers with glue.
4. Fill small containers with sunflower seeds.
5. Write child's name on sunflower picture.

procedures

1. *Introduction:* Recognizing, by name, the other children in the group is an ongoing objective of these lessons. To add fun to this objective, cut and paste a large sunflower on a cardboard backing. "Hide" behind the flower and have children guess who is hiding. Continue around the activity table having each child take turns "hiding" while others guess who is hiding.
2. Recall previous sunflower lessons with dried sunflower and fresh sunflower.
3. Demonstrate activity:
   a. Brush Elmer's glue into center of flower and sprinkle seeds into the glue.
   b. Brush glue on some outlined petals and stick yellow cut-out petals to glue.
4. Pass materials to children one item at a time and proceed with activity one step at a time.
5. Lay sunflower pictures flat until they dry.

problems

Some children may have difficulty placing seeds only in the middle. Encourage them to push seeds into the middle to make room for the petals.

adaptations

Some children may find it easier to do all the gluing in one step.

hints to maximize benefits

You may want to outline in green the stem and leaves of the sunflower if you include these in your picture; or you can include the stem and leaves as part of your pasting activity. Prepare and dry the completed sunflower project ahead of time as a demonstration for the children.

developmental processes

· Practice recall
· Reinforce name/person recognition
· Reinforce fine motor skills
· Practice eye-hand coordination
· Follow verbal and visual demonstration
· Practice social interaction skills

nature concepts and processes

· Sunflowers have seeds.
· Flowers have petals and seeds.

vocabulary

· *sunflower* · *seed* · *petals* · *yellow* · *stem* · *names* · *center* · *middle*

lesson 28   Transplanting Micro-Tom Tomatoes

Children will be able to harvest the fruit of the plants.

materials

Micro-Tom tomatoes in cell packs about 2″ high, soil, basins or trays, plastic serrated knives, scoops, 5″ standard pots, watering cans with water, saucers, dibbles, permanent marker, labels, store-bought cherry tomatoes.

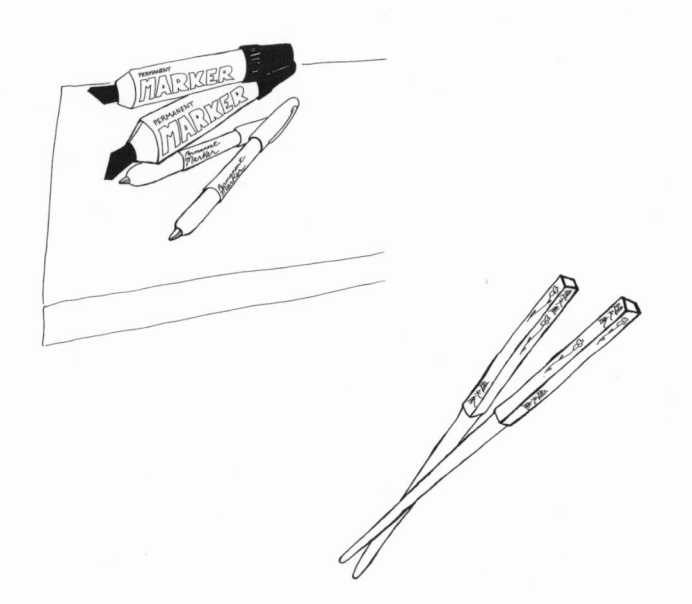

preparation

For each child:

1. Place approximately 1 qt. of soil in basin or tray.
2. Write label.
3. Draw line inside 5″ pot about 2″ below regular soil line.
4. Prepare area for transplanting activity.

procedures

1. *Introduction:* Introduce the transplanting lesson by comparing the sizes and shapes of different varieties of tomatoes; e.g., plum, cherry, salad. Each child can choose a tomato and slice it open with a plastic serrated knife and discover the seeds inside.
2. Pass cherry tomatoes to children and have them identify and taste the fruit.
3. Explain that most tomato plants grow outdoors because of the size of the plant and growing conditions, but that Micro-Tom tomatoes can grow on a sunny windowsill inside because they do not get very large.
4. Demonstrate transplanting activity:
   a. Show children where the soil line is drawn inside the pot with a marker.
   b. Fill standard pot with soil and press to firm with an empty pot.
   c. Make a large dibble hole in the middle and place the seedling in

the hole so that the roots are below the soil line and the plant is above the soil line.

    d. Place transplanted tomato pot into the saucer, and water and label it.

5. Have children complete activity as demonstrated.

horticultural requirements

Micro-Tom tomato seeds can be bought from Tomato Growers Supply Co., Fort Myers, Florida. To have a viable plant for the children to transplant, the tomatoes must be propagated about one month prior to the activity. Follow the directions on the seed package. Remember that all tomato plants need sun. Do not allow the plants to dry out. If deprived of water, they will produce less fruit and become susceptible to insect infestation.

problems

Tomato seedlings can be difficult for children to transplant if the seedlings are too small. If the seedlings are about 2"-3" high, they should have good root development and can be more easily handled by the children when removed from the cell packs. Have the children handle the plants by the root ball to avoid breaking the stem. Have extra plants available to ensure success.

adaptations

If you do not have cell packs to start seedlings, plant your seeds in empty egg cartons.

hints to maximize benefits

Tomatoes can be transplanted in the spring or early summer. If you are transplanting in the summer, and you want to have a mature plant to show the children, start your seedlings in early March. Follow seed package directions to determine time of maturity. When the fruit of the Micro-Tom tomato has matured, have each child cut open a tomato and identify the seeds.

developmental processes

· Compare sizes, shapes
· Follow sequential steps
· Reinforce motor and sensory skills
· Practice communication and social skills

nature concepts and processes

· Plants give us food to eat.
· Plants need water and sun to grow.
· Tomatoes come in many sizes and shapes.
· Tomatoes have seeds inside.

vocabulary

· *tomato* · *seedlings* · *red* · *seeds* · *roots* · *leaves* · *stem*

lesson 29   Transplanting Flowering Geraniums

This lesson can be combined with Lesson 40, *Making Gift Tags with Pressed Flowers.*

materials
Geranium plants in cell packs in bud and flower, soil, basins or trays, scoops, 4″ or 5″ standard pots, saucers, water in watering cans.

preparation
For each child:
1. Place approximately 1 qt. of soil in basin or tray.
2. Write name of child as well as plant name on pot.
3. Prepare activity area.

procedures
1. *Introduction:* Transplanting a geranium in flower gives children the instant satisfaction of knowing that they have completed a project successfully. Geraniums are in abundance in garden centers in the spring and you can offer the children many choices of colors. This activity not only reinforces what children have learned horticulturally (plant part identification), it also encourages social interaction as the children discuss to whom they will give the plant.

2. Have children identify parts of plant, especially flowers, and identify colors of flowers.
3. Demonstrate activity:
   a. Remove geranium plant from cell pack by squeezing.
   b. Put approximately 1″ of soil into pot (soil level should be at ridge line of pot, approximately 1″ below the rim).
   c. Place geranium into pot and add soil around plant to firm.
   d. Place transplanted pot into saucer, and water.
4. Have children pass soil basins around table.
5. Pass pots from one child to the next, encouraging them to use the person's name.
6. Encourage them to pick a plant and handle properly, keeping root ball intact.
7. Have children complete activity as demonstrated.

problems
Because children have completed many successful activities of planting and transplanting, they are familiar with materials. However, some children will require one-on-one assistance.

horticultural requirements
Geraniums need a sunny windowsill to grow. They like to get slightly dry between waterings.

hints to maximize benefits

Geraniums can be bought in inexpensive cell packs in garden centers in the spring. This activity is especially meaningful around Mother's Day. Decorate potted geraniums for gift giving. Use foil to wrap pots. For gift-tag enclosure, see Lesson 40, *Making Gift Tags with Pressed Flowers.*

developmental processes

- Practice multi-step directions
- Identify colors
- Identify parts of plants
- Practice making a choice
- Develop fine motor skills
- Practice gentle touch
- Practice social and communication skills
- Stimulate tactile, visual, and olfactory senses

nature concepts and processes

- Plants need soil and water.
- Plants have stems, flowers, and roots.
- Flowers can have different colors.
- Plants can be transplanted into a bigger container or pot.

vocabulary

- *geranium* · *color names* · *cell pack* · *squeeze*

lesson 30 Planting Grass Seeds

If planting space is available and accessible, seeds can be sown directly into prepared soil outdoors.

materials

Grass seeds, water tubes, soil, basins or trays, scoops, watering cans with water, saucers, permanent markers, labels; 4″ pots, citrus or pumpkin seeds, plastic wrap, 4″ azalea pot of germinated seeds.

preparation

For each child:

1. Write a label including child's name on one side and "grass seeds" on the other.
2. Fill water tubes with seed and secure with a lid. Cut a hole big enough to allow seeds to shake out easily.
3. Draw a line inside the pot about $1^{1}/_{2}$″ from the rim to indicate the soil level.
4. Fill the watering cans with a small amount of water so children will not wash out seeds when watering.
5. Prepare activity area.

procedures

1. *Introduction:* Plant propagation using seeds is repeated throughout the curriculum. This repetition reinforces learning. Germinate pots of grass seeds in preparation for this lesson. (Plant at least 3 weeks ahead of time so that the seeds can establish roots and leaves.) Introduce this lesson by examining grass pots. Identify the plant parts before continuing.
2. Ask children to hold out one hand, and place a small amount of seed in each hand.
3. Talk about the material in their hands and compare with citrus or pumpkin seeds (size, shape, texture).
4. Demonstrate how to plant seeds:
   a. Fill pot with soil and pack down to the line.
   b. Sprinkle with seeds.
   c. Cover with about $^{1}/_{2}$″ of soil.
   d. Water carefully and label.
   e. Put plastic wrap over pot.
5. Pass materials to children and complete activity.

problems

Just as with the activity of planting pumpkin seeds, take the opportunity to demonstrate to the children that the seeds will be washed away if the pot is overflowing. Explain that the seeds must be in the soil to grow.

adaptations

Do not overfill the watering cans. Watering cans should be filled with just enough water to saturate the soil.

hints to maximize benefits

Set pots in a warm place, but not in direct sun. When the seeds germinate, remove plastic and set in sun. Keep grass moderately moist. Transplant grass seed plugs outdoors if growing space is available.

developmental processes

· Compare shapes, sizes, and textures
· Follow directions
· Practice control of fine motor skills

nature concepts and processes

· Grass grows from seeds.
· Seeds are different sizes, shapes, and textures.
· Fast-flowing water will wash away soil and seeds.

vocabulary

· *grass* · *seed* · *roots* · *green*

lesson 31   Planting Seeds in Plastic Eggs

This activity can be combined with Lesson 30, *Planting Grass Seeds*.

materials

White plastic eggs, fresh eggs, water-based markers, small clay pots to hold eggs; scissors, glue gun, plastic container to hold small amount of soil, small plastic spoons, soil; sprout seeds (alfalfa/wheat/broccoli), water tubes to hold seeds and water (separately), plastic wrap; prepared sample of completed project.

preparation

For each child:

1. Cut a small opening in top of plastic egg with scissors to allow room for the soil.
2. Puncture a hole in the bottom for drainage.
3. Spread glue inside the circumference of clay pot and place prepared egg in pot.
4. Set aside to dry and check to make sure the eggs are secure.
5. In a small container, place 1 to 2 cups of soil.
6. Fill water tube with water and secure with lid. Cut a hole in lid big enough to allow water to flow.
7. Fill water tube with seeds and secure with lid. Cut a hole in lid big enough to allow seeds to flow easily when shaken.

procedures:

1. *Introduction:* In spring the world around us awakens. If you have the opportunity, take the children outdoors and observe the changes. You do not need an outdoor garden to see what is happening. Use what is accessible to you and the children.
2. Roll uncut white plastic eggs to children. Bounce them on the table and identify them as plastic eggs.
3. Have the children crack open real eggs into a basin and note the difference. (Don't worry about the mess; that's part of the fun.)
4. Show children decorated egg head in a pot and note where seeds are growing.
5. Collect the plastic eggs from children.
6. Pass a prepared clay pot with glued egg head to each child. Write child's name on the bottom of clay pot.
7. Pass water-based markers and have children decorate and color eggs and pot.
8. Collect the pens and pass soil and spoons.
9. Have children fill egg halfway with soil (indicate with marker ahead of time).
10. Pass seed tubes and have children sprinkle seeds in soil.
11. Cover seeds with soil.
12. Collect tubes with seeds and soil.

13. Pass watering tubes and have children water.

14. Cover egg with plastic and put in warm place to germinate.

problems
Using water tubes will solve the problem of over-watering.

adaptations
Plastic eggs can be set into egg cartons if you do not have small clay pots. Egg-shaped plastic containers, such as those used to hold pantyhose, can also be used. Make sure there is drainage.

hints to maximize benefits
Place seed tubes and watering tubes into a sheet of Styrofoam for easy handling. Place germinated egg head in a round pot.

developmental processes
· Practice fine motor skills
· Practice attending to task
· Compare plastic and real eggs
· Practice communication and social skills

nature concepts and processes
· Seeds grow in soil.
· Seeds need water to grow.
· Real eggshells can break easily.
· Plastic eggshells are hard to crack.

vocabulary
· *seeds* · *sprouts*

lesson 32　Holiday Nut Baskets

This horticulture craft activity continues to enrich the children's knowledge of seeds.

materials

Baskets approximately 5″ in diameter by 3″ height, Styrofoam 2″ thick; assorted nuts, pine cones, dried seed pods, water-soluble glue such as Elmer's in squeeze bottles; plastic containers to hold material, nutcracker or hammer for opening nuts, labels and permanent marker.

preparation

For each child:

1. Line the bottom of each basket with a piece of Styrofoam, making sure it is secure by wedging it into basket.
2. Fill each container with assorted nuts and other material.
3. Make sure squeeze bottles of glue are not blocked with dried glue.
4. Write label with child's name.
5. Prepare activity area.

procedures

1. *Introduction:* Whether children like or dislike peanut butter, most know what it is. Use this familiar food to help children discover that nuts are seeds in hard shells. Examine peanuts in shells, crack open the shell, and smell and taste. Continue the lesson with other nuts.

2. Pass nuts to each child and compare sizes, colors, shapes, and textures.
3. Crack open nuts one at a time and examine the seeds.
4. Discuss seeds for eating, seeds for planting, and using seeds for decoration.
5. Demonstrate activity:
   a. Fill basket with assorted nuts, pine cones, seed pods, etc.
   b. Squeeze glue over materials in basket to secure.
   c. Set aside to dry.
6. Pass assorted materials to children and encourage them to fill their baskets.
7. Proceed with gluing and labeling and set aside until dry.

problems

One-on-one assistance may be necessary for children to squeeze glue bottle.

adaptations

If you do not have individual squeeze bottles for glue, put glue into small Styrofoam or plastic dishes and have children spoon glue over the material.

hints to maximize benefits

You can decorate baskets for a special holiday with novelties from a craft store (e.g., snowmen, Santas, turkeys, Pilgrims). Compare nuts (seeds) for baskets to seeds that the children are familiar with (e.g., pumpkin and citrus seeds).

developmental processes

· Compare sizes, colors, shapes, and textures
· Stimulate olfactory and taste senses
· Practice fine motor skills
· Use social and communication skills

nature concepts and processes

· Nuts are seeds.
· We can eat seeds, and so can birds.
· Seeds and nuts come in many shapes, colors, sizes, and textures.
· Nuts have hard shells.

vocabulary

· *pine cones · nuts · seeds · shells · nutcracker*

lesson 33 Painting Pine Cones

This lesson combines natural materials with the creative and fun process of painting.

materials

Pine cones with flat tops (the larger the cones, the better), white water-based paint, brushes large enough for painting; small Styrofoam dishes, newspaper (to contain paint mess), pine cones of different sizes, pine boughs with cones attached; snow if available, other leaves to compare to pine needles (which also are leaves).

preparation

1. Put small amount of white paint into dishes.
2. Prepare activity area.

procedures

1. *Introduction:* With daylight hours getting shorter and shorter, we can still look to the winter garden for horticulture activities. Bring in pine boughs with pine cones attached. Examine the needles (leaves) and feel the stickiness of the stem. Feel the hardness of the cones. Explain that the cones produce seeds. Smell the pine scent.
2. Compare sizes of pine cones with children.
3. Demonstrate activity: Paint pine cone with white paint to look like snow.
4. Pass materials to children one item at a time and proceed one step at a time.

problems

Children may need some type of smock to protect clothing.

adaptations

Water-based paint of other colors can be used to paint the cones.

hints to maximize benefits

This is a two-day horticulture project. Have the finished product available for children to see. Have pine nut seeds (pignoli nuts) for children to touch and taste. Be careful of tasting if any children have problems with chewing and swallowing.

developmental processes

· Practice communication skills
· Stimulate olfactory and tactile senses
· Exercise fine motor skills
· Practice attending skills
· Compare shapes, textures, sizes, patterns

nature concepts and processes

· Pine cones grow outdoors on pine trees.

· Pine needles are leaves.

· Pine sap is sticky.

· Pine cones have many seeds inside.

vocabulary

· *pine cone · white paint · leaves · stem · sticky · needles · hard*

lesson 34　Creating Pine Cone Nests

This horticulture craft activity is especially appropriate for a holiday decoration.

materials

Pine cones, ribbon or roping, glue sticks and glue gun, small nuts and very small pine cones from hemlocks; small manufactured birds, floral sticky tape, Spanish moss, small Styrofoam dishes.

preparation

1. Cut ribbon or roping into 8"–12" lengths—or whatever length you want for hanging decorations.
2. Hot glue ribbon or roping to opposite sides of pine cone.
3. Put assortment of small nuts and small cones into small dishes.
4. Cut floral tape into 1"–2" strips.

procedures

1. *Introduction:* Using materials for horticulture crafts is a wonderful way for children to learn about their natural environment. Refer to Lesson 33, *Painting Pine Cones*, to introduce this activity. Using horticulture crafts diversifies the curriculum and reinforces learning in another modality.
2. Show children finished decoration.
3. Discuss habitat of birds.
4. Demonstrate activity:
   a. Place floral tape strips on top of painted pine cone, covering the top.

b. Remove paper after securing tape firmly.

c. Place bird on tape, pressing to secure.

d. Put nuts and cones around bird on tape, pressing firmly.

e. Make a nest by tucking a small amount of Spanish moss around bird.

5. Pass material to children one item at a time and proceed one step at a time.

problems
This activity requires many steps and some children may be distracted by the variety of materials. One-on-one assistance may be needed to complete the activity. It is important to do one step at a time.

adaptations
If children have difficulty handling pine cones, set the cones in plastic pots to stabilize them while they are being decorated. If activity is too difficult for children to focus, skip demonstration and proceed with activity one step at a time.

hints to maximize benefits
If you do not have the time to wait for pine cones to dry (Lesson 33, *Painting Pine Cones*), you can do this activity using natural, un-painted cones. This activity is especially meaningful during holiday time, as children can take home a handmade decoration.

developmental processes
· Exercise ability to follow multi-step directions
· Practice attending skills
· Exercise fine motor skills
· Compare shapes and textures

nature concepts and processes
· Birds live in nests.
· Birds lay eggs.
· Birds raise their babies in nests.
· Pine cones come in many sizes.
· Pine cones contain nuts.
· Pine cones and nuts feel and look different.

vocabulary
· *pine cone · bird · nest · nuts · Spanish moss*

lesson 35　Making a Pine Cone Bird Feeder

Use this activity to help children become aware of their natural environment.

materials
Pine cones, plastic knives, peanut butter, small Styrofoam dishes, wild-bird seed, twist ties, tray to put bird seed into for rolling pine cones.

preparation
1. Cut twist ties 18"–24" long and secure around top of pine cones for hanging outdoors.
2. Put peanut butter into dishes.
3. Put seed into tray.
4. Prepare activity area.

procedures
1. *Introduction:* If possible, take the children outdoors in winter and help them discover how their environment has changed. (The leaves are no longer on many trees, flowers have stopped blooming, the air is colder, and perhaps the ground is frozen.) Talk about birds. Some birds fly to warmer places when it is cold, but some do not. They still need food. Food is harder to find in winter. Discuss and plan how the children can help feed the birds.

2. Demonstrate how to make feeder:
   a. Cover pine cone with peanut butter, using plastic knives.
   b. Roll pine cone in seeds.
3. Pass materials to children one item at a time and proceed one step at a time.

problems
Most likely, children will want to taste peanut butter. Make sure that none of the children has allergies or swallowing disorders. This can be a messy project but very rewarding. (The children are taking responsibility for feeding the birds.)

adaptations
Use lard or bacon fat if some children should not taste peanut butter.

hints to maximize benefits
Hang feeders outdoors with children where they can observe birds feeding. Send home with each child a "bird feeder" kit, which includes a pine cone, twist ties, and seeds in a sealable plastic bag with "how-to" directions so children can construct a feeder at home with family members and observe what happens when the feeder is hung outdoors.

developmental processes
· Practice fine motor skills
· Reinforce social skills
· Exercise olfactory and tactile stimulation

nature concepts and processes
· Many birds eat seeds.
· Birds need food in the winter.
· In winter it is cold outside.
· Nature looks different in winter.

vocabulary
· *pine cones* · *seeds* · *birds* · *peanut butter*

lesson 36 Making Grapevine Picture Frames

This horticultural activity is appropriate for any time of the year.

materials

4" grapevine wreaths (can be bought in craft supply stores), individual pictures of each child cut to fit on back of wreath; heavy construction or blotter paper, scissors, hot-glue gun with glue, small containers, ribbon, dried and preserved flowers.

preparation

For each child:

1. Take individual pictures of the children ahead of time with a Polaroid camera, or have them bring in pictures from home.
2. Cut out picture in a circular shape to fit on wreath.
3. Hot glue picture to wreath with picture showing through the center.
4. Cut out construction paper in approximately 4" circle and hot glue around back of picture. (Make sure to glue only around the circumference of the picture, since glue can affect the quality of the picture face.) Press paper backing on glue.
5. When glue is dry and cool, trim picture and backing to shape of wreath.
6. Tie colorful ribbon to top of wreath for hanging.

7. Cut a 1"–2" piece of floral tape and press it onto front of wreath where dried material will not hide picture.
8. Cut up dried flowers to sizes that will fit on the wreath and fill small containers with material.

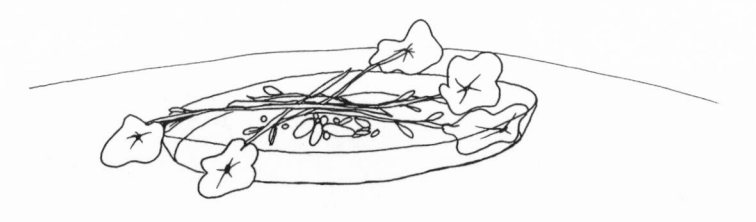

procedures

1. *Introduction:* Bring in fresh flowers and leaves and have children examine them. Press the flowers and leaves between 2 pieces of dark blotter construction paper to squeeze out water. Pass around the dried preserved flowers and leaves. Press and compare.
2. Demonstrate activity:
   a. Peel off paper to expose sticky floral tape.
   b. Gently but firmly press dried material to sticky tape.
3. Have children identify individual pictures.
4. Pass material one step at a time and proceed one step at a time.

problems

This is a labor-intensive project in terms of preparation for activity. Pictures can be taken over time and saved. Children love seeing their pictures and enjoy giving the grapevine wreath picture frame as a gift.

adaptations

Instead of using ribbon to hang the wreaths, use heavy magnetic tape secured across the back of the wreaths so they can be used as refrigerator decorations.

hints to maximize benefits

You can take pictures of children with a Polaroid camera and cut to fit wreath. Touch up the pressed flowers if necessary with a hot-glue gun after the children have decorated their wreaths. If you use magnetic tape, it is fun to hang the wreaths upside down on a metal can. Discuss why the pictures are not falling. Have the children take their own pictures off the cans.

developmental processes

· Practice visual and name recognition of others
· Reinforce fine motor abilities
· Practice social skills

nature concepts and processes

· Fresh flowers have water inside their leaves and petals.
· Flowers change their look and texture when dried.
· Magnets stick to metal.

vocabulary

· *flowers* · *wreath* · *wet* · *dry* · *colors* · *petals* · *stems* · *magnets*

lesson 37   Creating Fresh Green Centerpieces

Creativity abounds with this project.

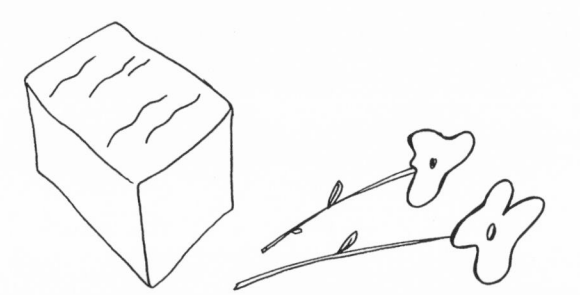

materials

Floral foam ("Oasis" is a familiar brand); garden greens including Euonymous, Arborvitae, Boxwood, and any other waxy garden material; 4" plastic containers, colorful foil or plant sleeves; serrated knife for cutting foam, basins, water, permanent marker, labels.

preparation

1. Cut chunks of floral foam to fit inside 4" container; foam should sit about $1/2$" above the rim of the plastic.
2. Cut the garden greens in uniform sizes 6"–8" long and remove bottom leaves from the stems.
3. Soak prepared foam in water-filled basins.

4. Write child's name on one side of label and the words "water daily" on the other.
5. Make a completed arrangement.
6. Prepare work area.

procedures

1. *Introduction:* Children love to water anything and introducing them to the properties of floral foam immediately holds their attention. When you are cutting the foam to fit into the plastic containers, you will have pieces you cannot use for arranging. Encourage the children to examine the dry foam. They will squeeze it and pull it apart. Put it in basins and have them "water" it. As it becomes saturated, note the changes: dry/wet; light/dark; light/heavy. Before starting the activity, caution the children against squeezing the foam for the arrangement. (Pressing compresses the air pockets and makes it difficult to push in the stems.) Have extra "leftovers" available for squeezing after the arrangement is complete.
2. Demonstrate how to put the stems into the foam:
   a. Have children participate by each taking a turn. Encourage them to put stems into the sides of the foam as well as the top.
   b. When turns are completed, hold the arrangement upside down to show that the greens are stationary and do not fall out.

c. Continue to fill spaces until area of foam is filled.

d. Water completed arrangement. Remind children that they must add water when they get home.

e. Place label in the foam on the side of the arrangements.

f. Place completed project in foil sleeve.

3. Have children choose a block of saturated foam and place it into their own plastic container. Make sure that the bottom of the foam is in contact with the bottom of the container (for its water supply).

4. Spread the pre-cut greens on trays and encourage the children to complete the arrangement as previously demonstrated.

5. When the children place the label with their name in the foam, remind them again to water every day.

6. Wrap each centerpiece in foil or in foil sleeve.

problems

One-on-one assistance may be necessary for children who are unable to push the stems into the foam.

hints to maximize benefits

You can plan to do this activity a number of times throughout the year. Your variety of materials will change with seasonal availability. Flowers are always an attractive addition, and sturdy stemmed flowers, such as mums, carnations, yarrow, and statice are recommended.

Children will have their own style of arranging. However, remind them to have the "face" of the flower look up. Discourage placing flowers so that they touch one another. It is advantageous to limit the number of flowers that each child may use.

Ribbon as well as novelties such as bunnies, bears, and seasonal signs like "Happy Mother's Day" can be bought in craft supply stores and used to embellish the arrangement.

developmental processes

· Exercise tactile and visual stimulation
· Follow directions
· Practice fine motor skills
· Practice multi-step directions and sequencing

nature concepts and processes

· Foam holds water like a sponge.
· Foam is light colored when dry.
· Foam is light in weight when dry.
· Foam is dark and heavy when wet.
· Flowers have faces that can turn up or down.

vocabulary

· *floral foam* · *dry/wet* · *light/heavy*
· *light/dark* · *face*

lesson 38 Building Birds' Nests

This project is especially meaningful when the children can collect some of the material needed to build the nest.

materials

There are many ways to approach this activity. Pre-constructed nests can be bought from craft stores, or small empty gift boxes can be used to hold a child-constructed nest. When collecting materials to build the nest, use your imagination and "think like a bird." Materials can include newspapers cut into strips, dried grasses, twigs and bark from trees, any kind of string and colorful ribbons, feathers, and lint from your clothes dryer.

preparation

1. Buy pre-constructed nests or small boxes to contain nests.
2. Buy plastic eggs and birds. Make sure that the eggs are large enough so that they cannot be swallowed by the children.
3. Collect all material for constructing nests.
4. Cut material into "nest-size" pieces.

procedure

1. *Introduction:* Abandoned nests are often visible for collecting when the trees are bare and the birds have flown to warmer climates. Find an abandoned nest if you can, and place it in a safe container so the children can handle it gently and look at it closely to observe what it is made of. Discuss what the object is (nest) and talk about what kind of animal (bird) could live in the nest. It is fun for the children if you place other animal replicas (plastic or wood) into the nest and ask if this is a possible home for a dog? a horse? an elephant? a giraffe?
2. Place the nest-building materials on the work table and have the children construct their own nests. Encourage them to use many different materials.
3. When the nests are completed, have the children choose plastic eggs and birds for their nests.
4. Have the children compare individual nests and the materials used.
5. Make different animal sounds. Have the children identify the sound with the animal (e.g., "moo" = cow). Have the children imitate the sounds a bird might make.

hints to maximize benefits

You might want to add "mud" to glue the nest together. Elmer's glue dyed with brown tempera paint and mixed with a little sand can be used as "mud." Before including this gluing activity in the lesson, make sure you practice so you know the preparation involved, drying time, and the results.

developmental processes

· Practice observation skills: compare, contrast, discriminate

· Reinforce fine motor and sensory abilities

· Practice making choices

· Practice social interaction and communication skills, including listening

nature concepts and processes

· Animals have homes; nests are homes for birds.

· Nests are constructed of different materials found by the birds.

vocabulary

· *nest* · *construct*

lesson 39   Pressing Flowers

This lesson is more meaningful after children have had experiences with identification of plant parts.

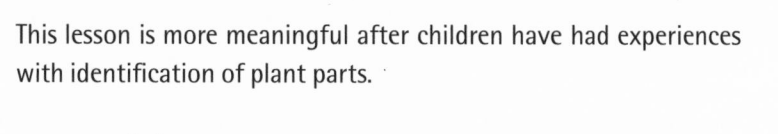

materials
Sponges, cut into small pieces, fresh flowers, trays, and flower presses, which can be bought from craft supply stores.

Use fresh flowers that are fairly flat with a single layer of petals, such as pansies, single hydrangea or azalea blossoms, baby's breath, and Queen Anne's lace. Ferns are also a good addition. Most leaves press well.

preparation
1. Buy or harvest flowers from the garden. Don't forget leaves.
2. Cut and remove stems.
3. Place on trays in a single layer.
4. Cut two pieces of blotter paper for each child and label with name.

procedures
1. Cut a small piece of wet sponge for each child and have them press the sponge between 2 pieces of dry construction paper.
2. Compare wet and dry.

MAKE YOUR OWN PRESS

You can build a homemade press using plywood squares approximately 8″ × 8″ with smoothed edges. You will need corrugated cardboard and blotting paper, cut to the same size. To secure the press, use a Velcro tape system bought at a craft or fabric store. Or you can drill holes in the four corners of the wood squares and insert 3″ bolts through the corner holes; use wing nuts to tighten (cut the corners off the cardboard and blotting paper to accommodate the bolts).

To press flowers, assemble the pieces in this order: bottom wood square, a piece of cardboard, a piece of blotting paper, a single layer of flowers and leaves, and another piece of blotting paper. Repeat layers to a height of 2 to 3 inches, and top with another piece of cardboard and the top wood square.

3. Explain that flowers and leaves contain water.
4. Compare pressed dry flowers and leaves with fresh flowers and leaves.
5. Demonstrate how to press flowers by placing plant material on blotter paper and following procedure above.
6. Have each child choose leaves and flowers to press. Make sure they don't overlap one another.

problems

Children may not be able to separate flowers on the blotter paper. Adjust their arrangements before assembling. One-on-one assistance may be necessary.

adaptation

You can also press flowers in a heavy old book. Make sure it has non-glossy pages.

hints to maximize benefits

Allow 3 to 6 weeks for the flowers and leaves to dry. They should feel like paper.

developmental processes

· Compare fresh and dry flowers
· Compare wet and dry
· Practice fine motor skills
· Compare shapes, forms, and colors
· Practice social and communication skills

nature concepts and processes

· Dry flowers last longer than wet ones.
· Flowers and leaves come in many shapes.
· Flowers and leaves contain water.
· Pressed flowers and leaves have dried out.

vocabulary

· *press* · *overlap* · *blotter* · *fresh flower* · *dry flower* · *cardboard*

lesson 40 Making Gift Tags with Pressed Flowers

This activity reinforces Lesson 39, *Pressing Flowers.*

materials
Empty flower press, flowers and/or leaves for pressing, dried flowers and leaves (pressed at an earlier time); blank paper note cards (approximately $3^1/_2'' \times 5''$), hole punch, scissors, ribbon, water-soluble glue, small brushes, small plastic or Styrofoam dishes.

preparation
1. Punch hole in corner of each note card.
2. Place dried material in small dishes.
3. Put glue into small dishes.
4. Cut fresh material into size for pressing.
5. Cut pieces of ribbon about 12″ long.

procedures
1. *Introduction:* If you have previously pressed flowers with the children in Lesson 39, open the press and discover what has happened. Use these flowers for the activity.
2. Demonstrate how a flower press works by having children place flowers and leaves on blotter paper and secure blotter paper with wooden top and press.
3. Compare fresh material with dried pressed material, noting the absence of water.
4. Demonstrate how to make a note card with pressed flowers:
    a. Brush glue onto note card.
    b. Press flowers and leaves onto cards, making sure that all material is on the card.
5. Pass materials to children one item at a time and complete activity one step at a time.
6. When glue has dried, pull ribbon through hole.

problems
This activity is really two separate activities, and the pressing of fresh material should be completed before making pressed flower gift tags. Have wet and dry paper towels handy for children to clean glue from fingers before handling dried material.

hints to maximize benefits
Press plant material all year long when available, (especially spring through autumn). Plant material takes weeks to dry. Use the gift tag to accompany a gift the child has completed (e.g., Mother's Day geranium).

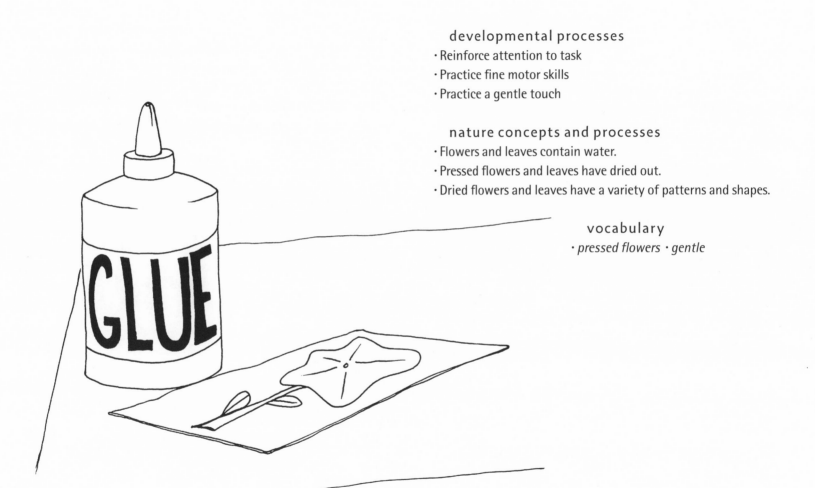

developmental processes
· Reinforce attention to task
· Practice fine motor skills
· Practice a gentle touch

nature concepts and processes
· Flowers and leaves contain water.
· Pressed flowers and leaves have dried out.
· Dried flowers and leaves have a variety of patterns and shapes.

vocabulary
· *pressed flowers* · *gentle*

GLOSSARY

accessibility

Design elements of an environment that facilitate ease of entry, movement, and participation.

adaptation

Modification of the process to make it more suitable for an individual student.

anoxia

Oxygen deprivation before, during, or after birth, which usually results in tissue damage that can be a cause or co-factor in many disabilities.

attending skills

Process of focusing on an activity.

cerebral palsy

A disability caused by damage to the brain before or during birth which can result in impaired muscular coordination, speech disturbances, or other motor or cognitive disabilities.

cognitive skills

Abilities relating to conscious intellectual activity such as thinking, reasoning, remembering, imagining, or learning language.

communication skill

Ability to exchange or transmit information between individuals.

coordination

The harmonious functioning of parts, as muscles and nerves, for most effective results.

dibble
A tapered stick-like device (e.g., a chopstick) used to make holes for planting.

Down's syndrome
A congenital condition characterized by moderate to severe cognitive, developmental, and physical disabilities.

dysplasia
Abnormal growth or development of tissues or body structures (e.g., hip dysplasia).

eye-hand coordination
Synchronization of visual and motor skills (e.g., reaching to grasp an object).

fine motor skills
Abilities relating to muscular movements of the arms, hands, wrists, and fingers.

gross motor skills
Abilities relating to large muscular movements of the body, such as walking, climbing, standing balance, stretching.

group process
Dynamics related to groups of people working together.

hand-over-hand
Process by which assistance is given to an individual by physically moving a part of the individual's body, usually a hand, in the correct motion to complete a task.

motor skills
Abilities related to muscle movements.

multi-step directions
A sequence of several one-step processes required to complete a task.

neurological impairment
Abnormal function of some aspect of the nervous system that coordinates and controls responses to stimuli, as in cerebral palsy or epilepsy.

olfactory sense
Related to the sense of smell.

orthopedic
Related to injuries, deformities, or diseases of the bones, joints, and muscles.

perceptual skill
Abilities related to awareness of the environment through sensory experiences.

recall
Remembrance of what has been previously learned or experienced.

sensory skills
Ability to interpret impulses experienced through the senses.

sensory-motor skills
Ability to function in both sensory and motor aspects of bodily activity.

sequencing
Combining individual steps to form a complete task or activity.

social interaction skills
Ability to communicate or interact with others in an understandable and appropriate manner.

spina bifida
Congenital disorder of the spinal cord that can cause a variety of disabilities.

succulent
A plant that has thick, fleshy tissues for storing water, such as a cactus.

tactile discrimination
Ability to interpret impulses experienced through touch.

tactile sensations
Physical experiences perceived by touch.

task analysis
Breaking down a step-by-step activity into its component one-step directions or parts.

textures
Qualities of a material that affect its appearance or the feel of its surface, structure, grain, etc.

therapy
Remedial treatment of a mental or physical disorder.

trauma
An injury caused by an outside agent.

visual discrimination
Ability to interpret impulses experienced through sight.

SUPPLIERS

The suppliers listed here answer the needs of owners of small, non-commercial greenhouses:

E. C. Geiger
(800) 4GEIGER (443-4337)
www.hortnet.com

Charley's Greenhouses
(800) 322-4707
www.charleysgreenhouses.com

GardenStyles
10740 Lyndale Avenue S., Suite 9W
Loomington MN 55420
(800) 356-8890

Jaderloon
P.O. Box 685
Irmo SC 29063
(800) 258-7171
Southwest: (800) 638-7670

X. S. Smith
Eatontown NJ 07724
(800) 631-2266

BIBLIOGRAPHY: NATURE/ENVIRONMENTAL EDUCATION PUBLICATIONS

Bremner, E. and Pusey, J.: *Children's Gardens*; Second Edition; 1990; University of California Cooperative Extension; Common Ground Program.

Elliot, P.: *The Garden and the Handicapped Child*; 1978; The Disabled Living Foundation, 346 Kensington High Street, London W14 8NS.

Gestwicki, Carol: *Developmentally Appropriate Practice: Curriculum and Development in Early Education*; Delmar Publishers Inc.; 1995.

Jurenka, N. A. and Blass, R. J.: *Beyond the Bean Seed: Gardening Activities for Grades K–6*; 1996; Teacher Ideas Press, Englewood CO.

Kite, P.: *Gardening Wizardry for Kids*; 1995; Barrons Educational Series, 250 Wireless Boulevard, Hauppauge NY 11788.

Life Lab Science: *Great Explorations*; 1992; Life Science Lab Program; University of California, Santa Cruz.

Miller, K.: *The Outside Play and Learning Book*; 1989; Gryphon House Inc., Mount Rainier MD 20712.

Milord, Susan: *The Kid's Nature Book*; 1989; Williamson Publishing, Charlotte VT.

Moore, R., Goltsman, S. and Iacofano, D.: *Play for All Guidelines*; 1992; MIG Communications, 1802 Fifth Street, Berkeley CA 94710.

National Gardening Association: *Grow Lab*; 180 Flynn Avenue, Burlington VT 05401.

Ocone, L.: *The Youth Gardening Book*; The National Gardening Association, 180 Flynn Avenue, Burlington VT 05401.

PLAE Inc.: *Universal Access to Outdoor Recreation*; 1994; MIG Communications, 1802 Fifth Street, Berkeley CA 94710.

Rockwell, R., Sherwood, E. and Williams, R.: *Hug A Tree*; 1986; Gryphon House Inc., Mt Rainier MD 20712.

University of California, Berkeley: *GEMS Publications Catalogue*; Lawrence Hall of Science #5200; Berkeley CA 94720-5200.

Wilke, Richard, Editor: *Environmental Education: Teacher Resource Handbook: A Practical Guide for K–12 Environmental Education*; 1993; Corwin Press, Inc., A Sage Publications Company, Thousand Oaks CA.

Wilson, Ruth, Editor: *Environmental Education at the Early Childhood Level*; 1994; North American Association for Advancement for Environmental Education (NAAEE), P.O. Box 400, Troy OH 45373.

Wilson, Ruth A.: *Fostering a Sense of Wonder During the Early Childhood Years*; 1993; OEEF, P.O. Box 1047, Columbus OH 43216.

Winnett, D., Rockwell, R., Sherwood, E. and Williams, R.: *Discovery Science*; 1996; Addison-Wesley Publishing Company, Innovative Learning Publications.

ABOUT THE AUTHORS

Stephanie L. Molen, a Registered Horticultural Therapist, has been on the staff of the Enid A. Haupt Glass Garden at Rusk Institute since 1993. Stephanie took the lead in designing and implementing the preschool nature curriculum. Her background includes teaching elementary school, training as a Master Gardener through Cornell Cooperative Extension, horticultural therapy training from the New York Botanical Garden, and training in floral design and botanical crafts. Stephanie emphasizes the elements of structure and sequential learning to enhance early childhood development.

Nancy K. Chambers, a Registered Horticultural Therapist, has been the Director of the Glass Garden at Rusk Institute since 1986. She is an aggressive proponent of the therapeutic value of nature in health-care environments. The many facets of the Glass Garden's programs, including the new Rusk Children's PlayGarden, reflect her conviction. She writes, lectures, teaches, and consults with programs here and abroad, and has received many distinguished honors for her work.

Matthew J. Wichrowski is a Registered Horticultural Therapist. He has been the Senior Horticultural Therapist and Conservatory Curator at the Glass Garden at Rusk Institute since 1993. With an affinity for research, Matt helps put the day-to-day clinical activities of the horticulture program in a theoretical framework. Matt is also active in developing the Glass Garden collections and Integrated Pest Management Program. He lectures at the New York Botanical Garden and Rutgers University.

Gwenn Fried is a horticultural therapist at the Glass Garden at Rusk Institute and BRC Adult Day Health Care, a day treatment program for people with AIDS. She is a Master Gardener with specialties in children's display, theme, and butterfly gardens. She is Director of Children's Events at Rutgers Gardens, lectures at Rutgers University and the New York Botanical Garden, and consults for Alzheimer's and Senior day-care programs in New Jersey. She is also the Glass Garden's computer "techie."